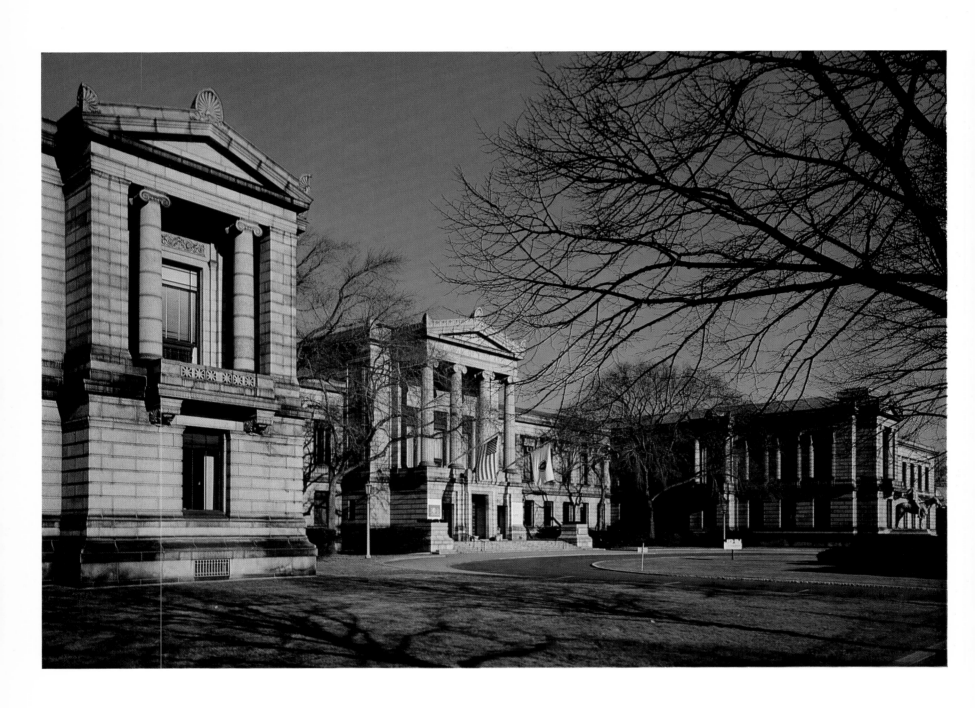

MUSEUM OF FINE ARTS BOSTON

ORIENTAL ART

Distributed by New York Graphic Society · Greenwich, Conn.

Jan Fontein

Pratapaditya Pal

Preface

WITHIN A FEW YEARS of the founding of the Museum of Fine Arts in 1870 and soon after it opened the doors of its first home in Copley Square in 1876, certain Bostonians were involved in serious pursuits in remote parts of the world which were to shape the destiny of the new institution. Forty years earlier, Egypt had been a goal of one such adventurer. Now it was Japan; soon it would be China, India, and other countries of Asia; then it would be Greece and Egypt again. The founders of the Boston Museum, without having a specific program, were actually engaged in a worldwide search for works of art that would be representative of all mankind. They were also laying the foundations of collections which were to gain world renown and secure for the fledgling institution a lofty position among museums everywhere.

Boston has always been an intellectual community, and it is not surprising that intellectual preoccupation should have found expression in the newly formed Museum. Indeed, the charter of the Museum provided for representation among the Trustees of three intellectual institutions: Harvard College, the Massachusetts Institute of Technology, and the Boston Athenaeum. Art as a luxury had limited appeal for nineteenth century Bostonians; nor were there in Boston the vast fortunes of the age to be found in other American cities which provided the means for such personal indulgence.

Instead, the motivation of these characteristic leaders of Boston was well grounded in intellectual curiosity, and their energies and ambitions redounded to the enrichment of their new institution. A sense of history inspired John Lowell to send back to Boston from Luxor as early as 1835 the first Egyptian monuments to come to America, works that became the nucleus of the Museum's great collection. Subsequently, archaeology attracted the support of the Trustees and led to the Museum's own expeditions in the Valley of the Nile. Similarly, it was the scholar who led the way to Japan, first the zoologist, Edward Sylvester Morse, followed by the professor of philosophy, Ernest Fenollosa.

From these early days to the present, the collections have been developed by men and women distinguished in their respective fields of learning. The Museum has attracted these scholars from Asia and Europe, as well as from our own country. Never have they relaxed the standards of quality established by the founders.

The works of art in the Museum today are the fruit of nearly one hundred years of effort. And they are testimony not only to the staff but to another distinguishing feature of the Boston Museum. From its inception, the Museum has depended almost entirely upon the gifts of private citizens. It is only within the past two years that it has had the benefit of any public support whatever. In this respect, it is unique among the great comprehensive museums in the world.

This volume is a testament to scholarly dedication and private benefaction joined together for the public good. It is also a measure of our present responsibility to conserve, display, and explain what is simply the greatest assemblage of Oriental art under one roof in the world; a brilliant cynosure for the scholar, the student, and the thoughtful man in a world smaller, narrower, and infinitely more complicated and delicate than the one which faced the Museum's founding fathers a century ago.

PERRY TOWNSEND RATHBONE

Early Japanese Sculpture in the Temple Room

Japanese Garden

Introduction

IT HAS OFTEN BEEN SAID that the Department of Asiatic Art of the Museum of Fine Arts in Boston has the finest collection of Oriental art under one roof in the world. This characterization is a sweeping as well as qualifying statement. None of the Museum's individual collections could be said to surpass that of the National Museum in the country where the works of art originated. Yet there is no other museum in the world in which the arts of India, Southeast Asia, and the Far East are represented together that can match the Museum's collections in size, scope and quality.

Before we proceed to sketch briefly the history of the Department of Asiatic Art, it is proper to comment on the circumstances which have led to the Museum's preeminence in the field of Oriental art. The high quality of the collection is due in part to the fact that it was begun at a time when art objects of great artistic merit were still in abundant supply. It has usually been taken for granted that Boston's great collections of Oriental art are a heritage of the China Trade, and the fact that several of the pioneers to whom we are indebted for our collections were indeed born in or lived at Salem, Massachusetts, one of the main ports of trade, would seem to bear out this supposition. Yet, upon closer scrutiny, it appears that the connection between the China Trade and the presence of such rich collections of Oriental art in Boston and vicinity may not have been as immediate as has often been assumed.

Like their predecessors of the European East India companies, the American mariners of the China Trade brought back to New England only what they could find in the ports: export porcelains, paintings on glass, ivory carvings, wallpaper, and some textiles. The great arts of China were created in the seclusion of the scholar's studio or in the workshops of the inaccessible Forbidden City. Therefore, the reason why the long history of early trading contacts between the Far East and New England did not result in the acquisition of Oriental art objects of first-rate importance by American collectors can be explained as a combination of limited understanding and lack of opportunity. Nevertheless, the China Trade may have contributed to the genesis of Boston's collections of Oriental art in quite a different way, something which becomes apparent when we compare events in Boston with what happened in Paris, where the vogue for things Japanese first developed.

To the French, who readily succumbed to the magic spell of *Japonisme*, Japan always remained a group of beautiful, distant islands, far beyond the horizon, to be admired from afar. With the exception of a few dealers, hardly any of the chief proponents of *Japonisme* ever set foot in Japan. Their romantic visions, mainly inspired by woodblock prints, were consequently denied the opportunity of confrontation with the true greatness of Japanese art and culture. Moreover, we may wonder whether they were really seeking such a confrontation, for *Japonisme* was, first and foremost, a reaction of artists who responded to the artistic message which they discovered in Japanese woodblock prints. Their interest was not directed toward Japanese art for its own sake, and did not extend beyond those aspects which they could use or adapt to their own artistic requirements. Thus, *Japonisme*, while it provided a lively source of inspiration for numerous great works of art and aroused a vivid interest in Japan among people all over the world, nevertheless did little of a substantial nature to stimulate real knowledge of Japanese art.

Unlike the French, to the inhabitants of New England, where the memory of the China Trade still lingered on, Japan was a tangible geographic reality, a country which could actually be visited if one were inclined to do so. Several of the Bostonians who were to play a prominent role in the vogue of things Japanese in Boston were in Paris when their first interest in Japan was awakened. However instead of continuing to admire Japan from afar, they considered it perfectly logical to make the voyage and see for themselves what Japan was like. This gave them an opportunity to establish their own criteria on a more pragmatic basis than the French had done. Their continuous exposure to the actualities of Japanese life and culture stimulated the development of different, higher standards of collecting and this resulted, within a very brief span of time, in the growth of great collections of Japanese art. However, there is yet another important difference between what happened in Paris and in Boston. Following the famous example of de Goncourt, who proclaimed that the best way of sharing his collection with the public was to have it auctioned and dispersed, practically all of the great collectors of Paris disposed of their collections during the first decade of this century. Although the auctions of the collections of Hayashi, Gillot, Bing, and others stimulated a brief *hausse* in Japanese art, they also marked the beginning of the end of *Japonisme* and soon, even in Paris, China replaced Japan in the favor of the collectors.

In Boston, on the other hand, the collectors of Japanese art seem to have had, from the very beginning of their activities in Japan, the idea that they should serve the public interest, and that this could best be done by buying these collections for or donating them to the newly founded Museum of Fine Arts in Boston. As a result, the most tangible and lasting product of the Japanese vogue in Boston—its great collections of Japanese art—was kept intact and what would otherwise have been merely a colorful interlude in the cultural history of New England became part of the early history of this permanent collection.

The scholars, collectors, and benefactors whose combined efforts resulted in the establishment and development of the Department of Asiatic Art were brought together through a series of happy coincidences. The first of these men to travel to Japan did not go in search of artistic beauty at all. Edward Sylvester Morse (1838–1925), a Harvard-trained zoologist, set off for Japan in 1877, his objective being to collect specimens of a species of marine fauna known as brachiopods. Morse was among the first foreigners to see Tōshōgu Shrine at Nikkō, now a major tourist attraction, but he hardly paid any attention to it, concentrating instead on the task of collecting shells on the shore of nearby Lake Chūzenji. On the second day after his arrival in Japan he took the train from Yokohama to Tokyo, and from the window he noticed that the recently built railroad cut through a group of large shell mounds. Returning to the spot soon afterwards, he conducted the first archaeological excavation in the history of Japan. The publication of his finds, *Shell Mounds of Omori* (1897), was the first scientific study published by the newly founded University of Tokyo.

Morse was highly systematic as a collector and well versed in the techniques of classifying and cataloguing. When he discovered the infinite variety of contemporary Japanese ceramics, he was fascinated and began to apply all of his great scholarly skills to assembling a representative collection. The final result of his efforts was an enormous collection numbering well over five thousand pieces. Systematically arranged according to provenance and kilns, they now fill dozens of crowded cases on the third floor of the Museum of Fine Arts. Even though the number of pieces of great artistic merit is not very large, the collection nevertheless contains a number of well-documented, important archaeological specimens and gives a most thorough and comprehensive view of practically all types of nineteenth century Japanese pottery.

Much more important, however, than Morse's contributions to the permanent collections of the Museum were the results of his influence on other Americans whom he persuaded to come to Japan. The first of these was Ernest Francisco Fenollosa (1853–1908), the son of a Spanish-born musician of Salem, Massachusetts, and a neighbor of Morse. He had just finished his studies at Harvard when he received an appointment as Professor of Philosophy at the University of Tokyo in 1878 at Morse's recommendation. Fenollosa arrived in Japan only one year after Morse, but he was drawn into the orbit of Japanese art much sooner than his mentor had been.

At the time of Fenollosa's arrival in Japan the prestige of traditional Japanese art had reached a low ebb. It was actually largely due to Fenollosa's energetic efforts that the Japanese gradually came to realize the importance of preserving the relics of their own ancient

11

culture. His important role in the revival of Japanese interest in their own artistic heritage need not be treated here. However, his many activities were not confined to teaching philosophy and propagating a revival of the traditional arts. Another of his projects can best be described in Fenollosa's own words, as he wrote them to Morse: "We have been through all the principal temples in Yamashiro and Yamato armed with government letters and orders, have ransacked godowns, and brought to light pieces of statue from the lowest stratum of debris in the top stories of pagodas 1300 years old. We may say in brief that we have made the first accurate list of the great art treasures kept in the central temples of Japan, we have overturned the traditional criticism attached to these individual specimens for ages. . . ."

The first of these excursions was undertaken in 1880. It seems to have whetted Fenollosa's appetite for collecting, an activity for which he was better qualified than any other Westerner of his time and for which he possessed unusual gifts. The most memorable souvenir of his first trip to Kyoto is the Matsushima screen by Kōrin (Pls. 25–26), now in the Museum of Fine Arts.

In 1882 Fenollosa made his third trip to Japan, accompanied by the Bostonian physician Dr. William Sturgis Bigelow (1850–1926), who was so fascinated by the country that he stayed on for seven years. He was immediately drawn into Fenollosa's circle and soon started to accompany him on his trips in search of hidden temple treasures. It was during one of these early excursions in 1884 that Bigelow was able to acquire the *Hokkedō Kompon Mandara* (Pl. 10), the only painting of the Nara period ever to leave the country. Although Dr. Bigelow became deeply interested in Tendai and Esoteric Buddhism, which he studied with great diligence, he also devoted much of his time to the collecting of Japanese art on a truly grand scale. He had a wide range of interests, and the great variety of important material assembled in his collection is an accurate reflection of the catholicity of his taste.

By the time Bigelow had determined that his collection should go to the Boston Museum, it already consisted of thousands of pieces. But he not only sent his own collection to Boston, he also persuaded his friend Charles Goddard Weld (1857–1911) to buy, in 1886, the entire collection of Ernest Fenollosa, which was sold with the understanding that it was to remain permanently in the Museum of Fine Arts. When it arrived in Boston in 1889, together with the Bigelow collection, and when the two collections were displayed in the course of the following year, the Museum of Fine Arts had clearly established the preeminence in the field of Japanese art which was henceforth to be one of its salient characteristics.

Whereas the Bigelow collection is made up of a great variety of Japanese works of art, the Fenollosa-Weld collection consists almost entirely of paintings. Although the Japanese collections were added to in later years, they still bear the imprint of Fenollosa's approach to Japanese art. Fenollosa's admiration for the Kano school—he was adopted by the Kano family and received the name of Kano Eitan—is reflected in his collection, which contains fine works of practically all leading masters of the school. Where his and Bigelow's interests ran parallel, as, for example, in their appreciation of the painter Soga Shōhaku (1730–1781) (see Pls. 59–60), the Boston collection is without equal. The inevitable consequence is, however, that those schools or masters whom Fenollosa did not appreciate are either poorly represented or almost totally lacking. This is particularly true of the Nanga or Bunjinga school, the works of which Fenollosa once characterized as "hardly more than an awkward joke". This resulted in a lacuna which we can now hardly hope to fill, but which we can easily forgive a man of such great taste and foresight.

Ernest Fenollosa arrived in Boston soon after the collection which bore his and Dr. Weld's name. In 1890 he was appointed Curator of the Japanese Department of the Museum of Fine Arts. The next four years were spent cataloguing and installing the collections and in organizing a series of exhibitions of Japanese art, from Japanese as well as from our own collections, which were undoubtedly the most significant held up to that time.

The last in this series of exhibitions was a traveling show of Lohan paintings from the Daitokuji, Kyoto. These paintings, dating from between 1178 and 1184 and the work of two painters, Chou Chi-ch'ang and Lin T'ing-kuei, are among the finest Chinese Buddhist paintings in existence. Bernard Berenson gave his future wife, Mary Costelloe, an eye-witness report of this exhibition: ". . . To begin with they had composition of figures and groups as perfect and simple as the best we Europeans have ever done . . . I was prostrate. Fenollosa shivered as he looked, I thought I should die, and even Denman Ross who looked dumpy Anglo-Saxon was jumping up and down. We had to poke and pinch each other's necks and wept. No, decidedly I never had such an art experience." It would be understandable if now, almost seventy-five years after the event, the objects of their highly emotional reactions failed to meet the fastidious art historical standards of our own times. However, that they were deeply moved by what are still considered creations of the highest artistic order can only increase our admiration for their early understanding and appreciation of Oriental art.

Before the exhibition returned to Japan, the Daitokuji sold ten of the paintings to the Museum of Fine Arts to pay for urgently needed temple repairs. It was one of the last services which Fenollosa was to render to the Department of Asiatic Art. Shortly afterwards the circumstances connected with his divorce and remarriage resulted in his leaving the Museum.

With the departure of Ernest Fenollosa the rapid growth of the collections seems to have slowed down, only to increase again with the arrival on the Boston scene of one of Fenollosa's most gifted Japanese pupils, Okakura Kakuzō (1862–1913). Okakura had accompanied Fenollosa on many of his excursions in search of temple treasures, sharing with him such exciting experiences as the discovery of the Yumedono Kannon (1884). Afterwards he had headed the new Fine Arts Academy, but in 1898 he resigned from this position as well as his post at the Imperial Museum, Tokyo. It was extremely fortunate for the Museum of Fine Arts that a person of such great talents was available and willing to lead the Department into what was soon to become another era of dynamic expansion.

Okakura Kakuzō was undoubtedly one of the greatest connoisseurs of Far Eastern art of his time, a man with a remarkably wide range of interests who was equally well versed in Chinese and Japanese art. Of his numerous writings, *The Book of Tea* and *Ideals of the East* were read and admired all over the Western world. But although his international fame rests upon these publications, the extraordinary talents of this versatile cosmopolitan are demonstrated even more clearly by the high quality of the additions he made to the collections of the Museum.

It could be said that Okakura tried to put into practice as a museum curator his own famous dictum, "Asia is one," for it was on his initiative that the collection, which consisted up to that time almost entirely of Japanese works of art, was first expanded into other fields of Oriental art. This is not to suggest that Okakura neglected the art of his native country. On the contrary, among his acquisitions for the Department are such works as the Landscape in Chinese style by Bunsei (Pl. 47) and a large group of wooden sculptures, of which the monumental Shō Kannon (Pl. 4) is one of an importance which has no parallel in any collection outside Japan. As early as 1893, however, Okakura had journeyed to China, and the art of that country had become an absorbing interest to him. Later, when he came to Boston, this predilection resulted in the first steps towards the assembling of a collection of Chinese art.

On his first trip to China, as on all of his later expeditions to that country, Okakura was accompanied by Hayasaki Kōkichi (1874–1956), the son of his step-sister. Hayasaki, a pupil of the painter Hashimoto Gahō, was an amateur archaeologist and an excellent connoisseur of Chinese art. For many years he lived in China, where he developed a deep interest in Taoism, associating with the priests of the Temple of the Eight Immortals at Hsi-an and adopting for himself their traditional costume. After Okakura had joined the staff of the

14

Museum of Fine Arts, Hayasaki became the Museum's agent in China. Among many other pieces, our unique collection of dated Taoist stone statues, the sarcophagus for the ashes of a Buddist patriarch of the Sui period (16.287), Ma Yüan's album leaf *Bare Willows and Distant Mountains* (Pl. 80) and, above all, the handscroll *Clear Weather in the Valley* (Pl. 79), formerly attributed to Tung Yüan, are the fruit of this collaboration.

However, for the rapid growth of the Chinese collections and the extraordinarily high quality of many of the new acquisitions, the discerning eyes of Okakura and Hayasaki should not be given exclusive credit. The unconventional, enlightened policy of the Museum regarding methods of acquisition, the harmonious collaboration between Japanese and Bostonians, between gifted scholars and discerning collectors, enterprising dealers and generous benefactors—all this should be taken into account. To recapture the atmosphere in which these men all worked together, nothing would seem to be more appropriate than to quote from a letter which Okakura's successor, John Ellerton Lodge, wrote to Hayasaki on August 18, 1916: "I am particularly anxious that, in prosecuting your labors for the Museum, you should be relieved as much as possible from any sense of constraint you may have regarding the prices you pay and the number of things you buy. To me it seems that if, for example, your last trip to China had yielded nothing more than the sarcophagus, you would be fully justified in priding yourself on your accomplishment, and the Museum would have ample grounds for satisfaction. This implies that we are interested primarily and above all in the quality of what we receive from you, and that the number of things you buy, their prices, and the ratio of those prices to your own expenses, are matter of secondary importance,—provided, always, that the things themselves are, as they should be, absolutely first-rate of their respective kinds."

The diligent search for excellence, of which this statement is an eloquent example, was clearly much more than the pastime of a few fastidious collectors who demanded and could afford the finest works of art. Okakura's genuine enthusiasm, and his ability to communicate this feeling, inspired in many others a unique dedication to the Department of Asiatic Art. In a world in which the appreciation of Oriental art was, as yet, restricted to only a happy few, these men joined together to further the task of demonstrating that the arts of the Far East were in no way inferior to those of Egypt, Greece, Rome and the Renaissance. They felt that this objective could only be realized in a convincing manner if the works of art they assembled were of the highest artistic quality, and in order to reach this goal they were willing to make sacrifices of the sort which still command our deep admiration.

Edward J. Holmes was one of those whom Okakura inspired, and his dedication can

15

perhaps best be illustrated by the historic anecdote that he persuaded his mother to borrow money—for the first time in her life—in order to purchase the Tuan Fang altar group of the Sui period (Pl. 93). Equally dedicated, and endowed with a remarkably visionary capacity, was Denman Waldo Ross (1853–1935) who served as a Trustee from 1895 until his death. He played an important role in the development of the Department. It was he who rediscovered in Paris the long-lost stone sculpture from the White Horse Monastery in Loyang (Pl. 63), which Okakura had tried in vain to buy in 1906. The news of its rediscovery did not reach Okakura before his death, and Ross purchased the piece himself and gave it to the Museum in memory of his friend.

It was at the initiative of Dr. Ross that the Museum branched out into yet another field of Oriental art. Just before the outbreak of the First World War, skillfully conducted negotiations led to the acquisition for the Department of the entire collection of Indian and Persian miniatures of Victor Goloubew. Further progress in this direction was made during the curatorship of John Ellerton Lodge, who became curator in 1915 and who, from 1921 to 1931, held this position concurrently with that of Director of the newly founded Freer Gallery of Art in Washington, D.C. In 1917, when Dr. Ross made one of his frequent generous gifts to the Museum, he included a large collection of Indian art which had been assembled by Ananda K. Coomaraswamy (1877–1947). Here history repeated itself, for just as Ernest Fenollosa had become curator of his own collection after it had been bought for the Boston Museum by Dr. Weld, so Ananda Coomaraswamy followed his own collection to Boston after it had been given to the Museum by Dr. Ross. Thus, the Museum acquired not only an outstanding collection of Indian art, but also the most brilliant scholar in the field of Indian art of his time. Coomaraswamy remained in Boston for the rest of his life and many of the books of this prolific genius, who contributed so much to our understanding of Indian art, were written in the Museum.

Another important accomplishment which took place during the curatorship of John Ellerton Lodge was the purchase from the heirs of Okakura of a number of works of art from the late curator's private collection, assembled in the years prior to his association with the Boston Museum. Seven years after Okakura's death, the Museum was able to acquire the painting representing Dai-itoku Myō-ō (Pl. 9) and the statue of Miroku by Kaikei (Pl. 6), two of the greatest masterpieces of Japanese art in the collection.

In 1931, when Lodge decided to devote himself entirely to the directorship of the Freer Gallery, Kojiro Tomita, a disciple of Okakura Kakuzō, became his successor. Tomita had joined the staff of the Museum in 1907 at the age of eighteen and he retired as curator in 1962, the longest term of service in the history of the Museum. The period of his curatorship was marked by a long succession of brilliant acquisitions made possible in part by the munificence of a new generation of benefactors. The new curator did not follow the fashionable trend in buying of the thirties, which saw the rapid growth of collections of Chinese bronzes in Japan, in Europe, and in America. While the few bronzes which were bought are of rare distinction, such as the Mongolian Youth (Pl. 61), no major effort was made to compete with other museums for the many excellent bronze vessels excavated in China during those years. Instead, the Museum concentrated its limited resources on a determined effort to expand the collection of early Chinese paintings. Hui-tsung's *Five-colored Parakeet* (Pl. 70) and Yen Li-pên's *The Thirteen Emperors* (Pls. 67–69) are the crowning achievement of this far-sighted policy. After the Second World War the emphasis in the Department's acquisition program was shifted to Ming and Ch'ing paintings. This successful policy was largely made possible by the generous bequest of Keith McLeod in 1956.

The scope of the collection was once more expanded in a spectacular way when Charles Bain Hoyt (1889–1949) bequeathed to the Museum his large collection of Oriental art, chiefly of Chinese and Korean ceramics. All types of early Chinese ceramics, with the exception of Chün and Kuan wares, are represented in this collection, each with several choice specimens. As early as the First World War, Charles Hoyt had become interested in Korean celadons, a field then largely ignored by collectors of Oriental ceramics, and it is due to Hoyt's enlightened attitude that the Museum now has one of the finest collections of Korean ceramics in the world (see Pls. 89–90).

When Robert Treat Paine succeeded to the curatorship in 1962 after many years of service to the Department, the possibilities for adding works of art of the quality of those previously acquired had been greatly reduced. Although chiefly known as an expert on Japanese prints, his remarkable connoisseurship of Japanese painting is evident from the purchases he made as a young student in Japan. The triptych by Tōyō (Pl. 55), which he acquired at the auction of the collection of the Bishamondō Temple, Kyoto, and which he gave to the Museum many years later, is one of the last great masterpieces of Japanese painting to enter the collection. Paine's tragic and premature death, only two years after he had become curator, left him no time to carry out his plans for the future of the Department. Moreover, the changes in the political climate and the laws restricting the export of important art objects from many countries in the Orient have greatly reduced the possibilities for adding to the collection works of art of a quality comparable to that of those acquired in the past. It may be said, therefore, that the collection in all probability will retain essentially its present form.

The present publication is a first effort to introduce the Asiatic collection to a wider public by means of a selection from the Museum's masterworks. In a brief survey such as this, it is impossible to do justice to all facets of the collection and to the numerous benefactors whose generosity has made the Museum of Fine Arts into the great institution which it is. Important parts of the collection, such as the Japanese printroom (which contains more than 50,000 Japanese woodblock prints) have not been treated at all in this publication, and this necessitated the omission of more than a passing reference to the gift of William S. and John T. Spaulding, whose magnificent prints, often still in prime condition, can only be shown to visitors upon request.

Although two members of the staff of the Department are responsible for the explanatory texts, many more have contributed to this work. Hsien-ch'i Tseng, Money L. Hickman and Chimyo Horioka, members of the present staff, have made many valuable comments and proposed a number of improvements. Moreover, the authors have drawn freely upon the wealth of facts and opinions which have accumulated in the files of the Department and which represent the outcome of many years of research by previous generations of staff members and visiting scholars. The publication of this book, in close cooperation with Kōdansha, Ltd., is a typical result of the close ties with the countries of the Far East on which the Department has prided itself during all the years of its long history.

JAN FONTEIN

I Japanese Art

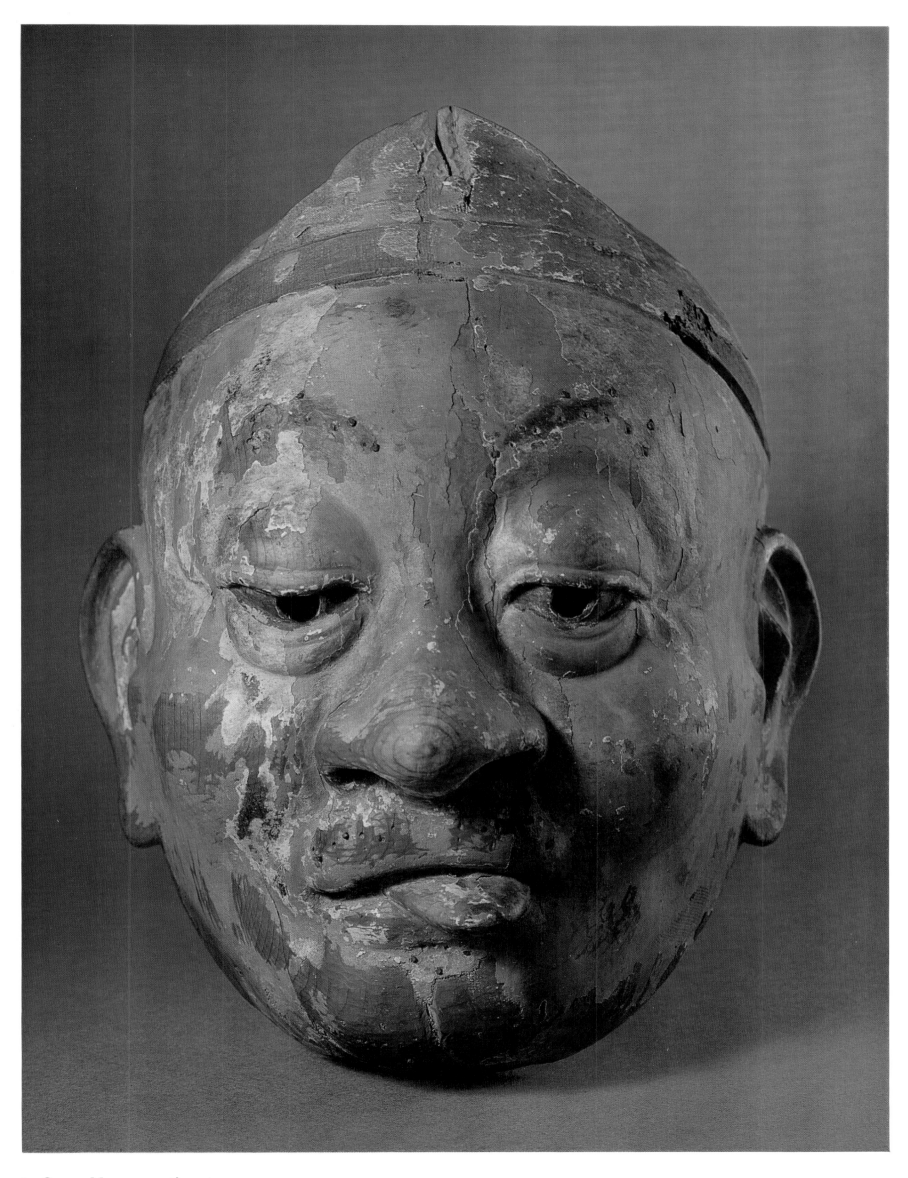

1 Gigaku Mask   ca. 11th century

2 ŚĀKYAMUNI late 10th century

3 DAI-ITOKU MYŌ-Ō (detail) 10th–11th century

4 SHŌ KANNON
late 8th–early 9th century

5 Saichi Shō Kannon (Avalokiteśvara) A.D. 1270

6 **Kaikei** Miroku Bosatsu (detail) A.D. 1189

7 **Kōshun** Sōgyō Hachiman A.D. 1328

8 Hokkedō Kompon Mandara   late 8th–early 9th century

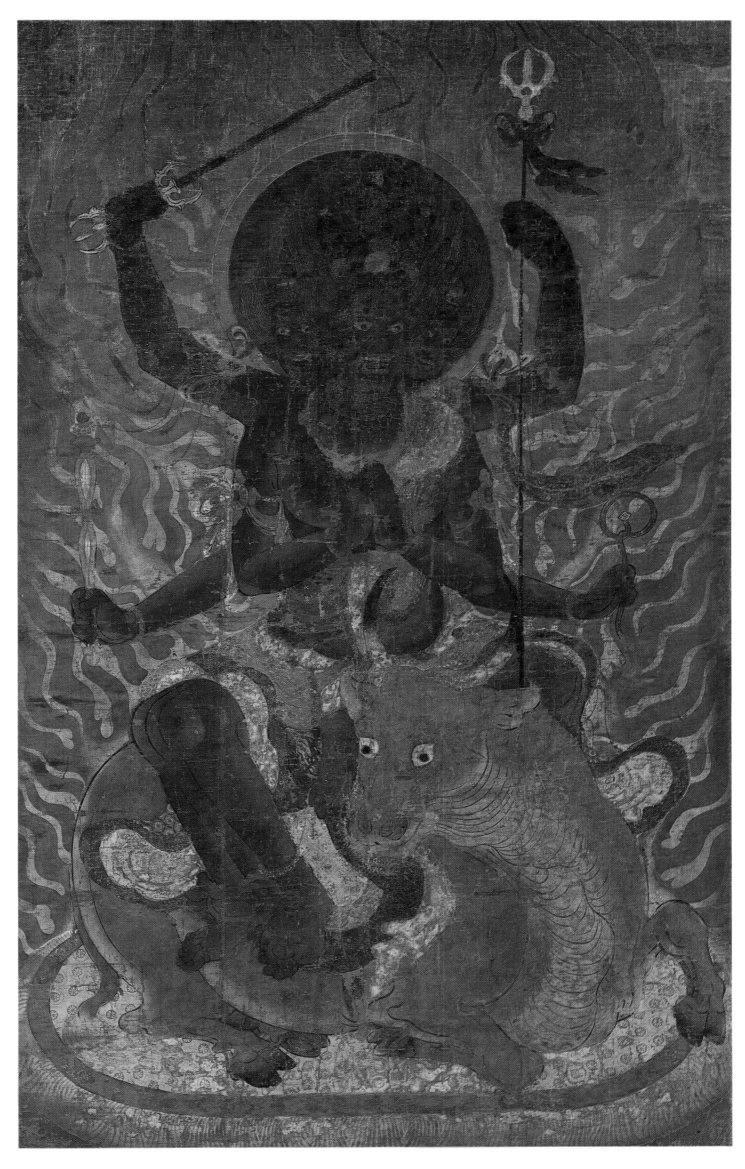

9 FUGEN EMMEI mid 12th century

10 Dai-itoku Myō-ō 11th century

11 BATŌ KANNON   12th century

12 DAINICHI as ICHIJIKINRIN late 12th century

13 Nyo-irin Kannon (detail) ca. A.D. 1200

14   Bishamonten Mandara   late 12th–early 15th century

15 Kɪʙɪ Dᴀɪᴊɪɴ Nɪᴛᴛō E-ᴋᴏᴛᴏʙᴀ (detail)   late 12th century

16–17 Kibi Daijin Nittō E-kotoba (details)   late 12th century

17

18   HEIJI MONOGATARI EMAKI (The Burning of the Sanjō Palace) (detail)   third quarter of the 13th century

19–20 Heiji Monogatari Emaki (The Burning of the Sanjō Palace) (details)   third quarter of the 13th century

20

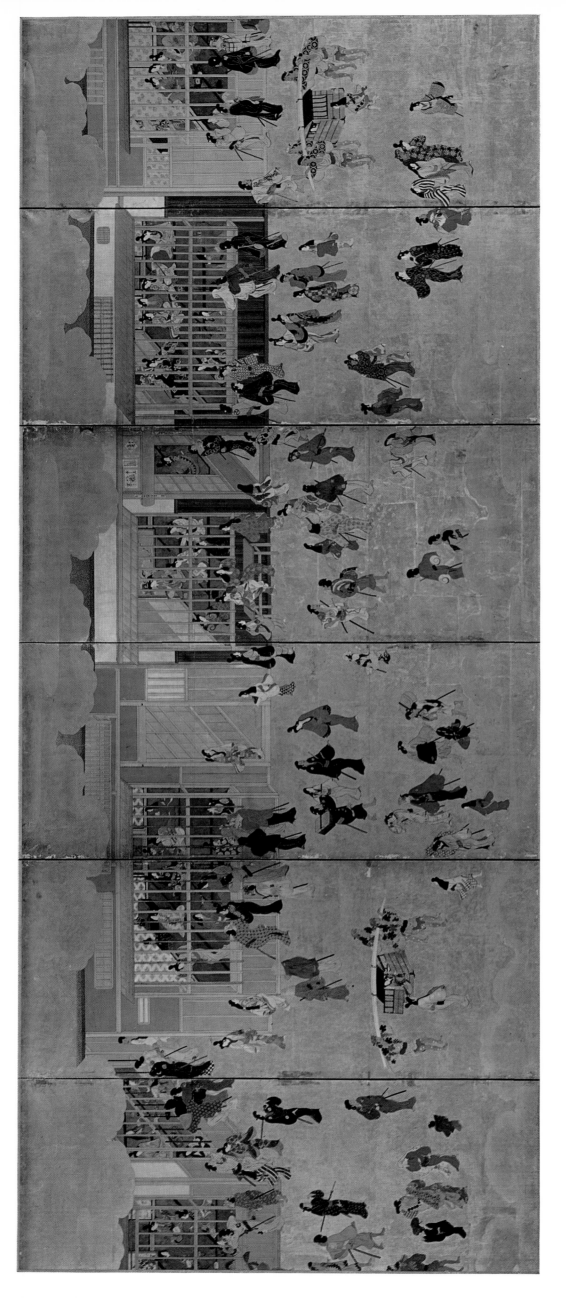

21–22   The Gay Quarters of Kyoto   second half of the 17th century

23–24 THE GAY QUARTERS OF KYOTO (details) second half of the 17th century

24

25 **Ogata Kōrin** Matsushima (detail) early 18th century

26 Ogata Kōrin Matsushima early 18th century

27–28 Sōtatsu School POPPIES 17th century

29   EUROPEAN KING AND COURTIERS (detail)   early 17th century

30 THE ARRIVAL OF A PORTUGUESE SHIP IN JAPAN (detail)   early 17th century

31–32 A View of Shijō-Kawaramachi (details) mid 17th century

33 THEATER SCENES AT FUKIYA-CHŌ (detail)   late 17th–early 18th century

34 Mori Sosen MONKEYS (detail) late 17th century

35–36 Sōtatsu-Kōrin School SPRING AND AUTUMN FLOWERS first half of the 18th century

37 Torii Kiyonaga
A Mother and Daughter under a Willow Tree
late 18th century

38 ATSUITA KARAORI late 18th century

39 Vase Ko-Seto ware 14th century

40 DISH Shino ware early 17th century

41   DISH   Ko-Kutani ware   late 17th century

42 JAR Kakiëmon ware late 17th century

43 Tebako (Handy Box) 14th century

44 Suzuribako (Ink Stone Box) 17th century

45 Ogawa Haritsu BOX FOR WRITING PAPER 17th–18th century

46 School of Geiami Jittoku Laughing at the Moon late 15th century

47 **Bunsei** LANDSCAPE
ca. mid 15th century

48 Tan'an Chiden Night Heron
late 15th–early 16th century

49–50 **Zōsan** THE FOUR SEASONS early 16th century

51 Sesshū Monkeys and Birds in Trees A.D. 1491

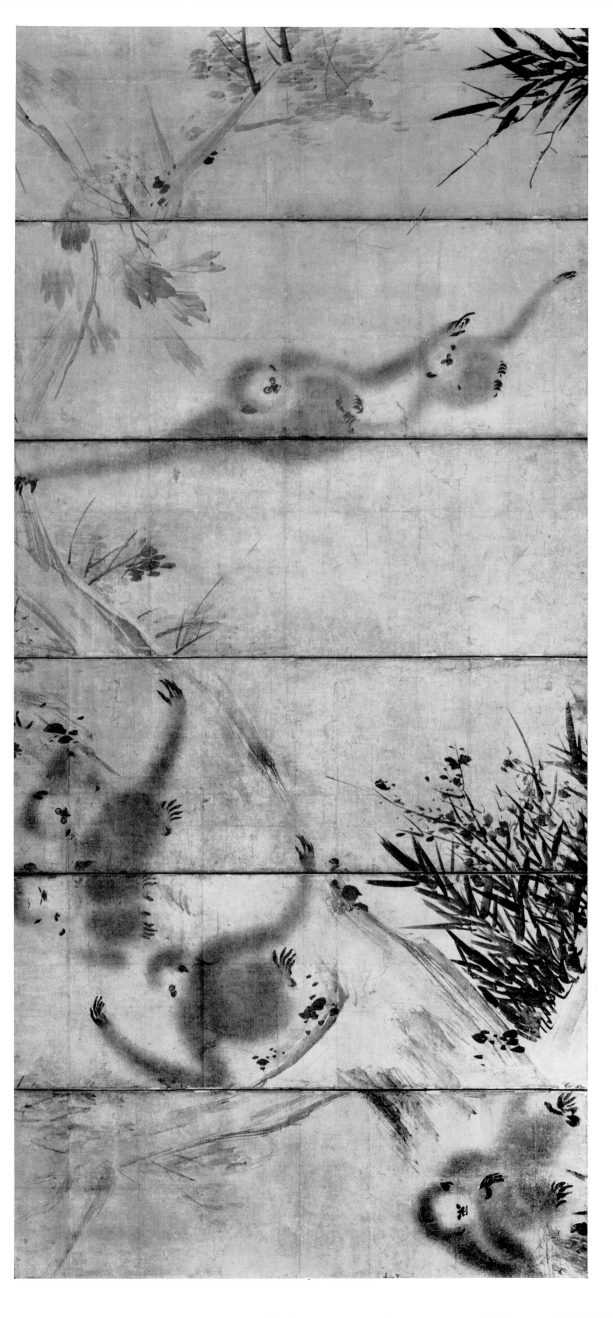

53 **Keishoki** LANDSCAPE late 15th–early 16th century

54 Attributed to **Kano Eitoku** TIGER 16th century

55 Tōyō THE THREE SAGES 15th century

56 Kano Tanyū CONFUCIUS AT THE APRICOT ALTAR 17th century

57–58   Uᴛᴀᴛᴀɴᴇ ɴᴏ Eᴢōsʜɪ (details)   16th century

59–60 **Soga Shōhaku** The Four Greybeards of Mount Shang 18th century

II Chinese and Korean Art

61 MONGOLIAN YOUTH   ca. 4th–3rd century B.C.

62 KUAN-YIN

ca. A.D. 580

63 BODHISATTVA
ca. A.D. 530

64 KUAN-YIN ca. 12th century

65 YAKSA YŎRAE ca. 8th century

66 ANIMAL FIGHT IN THE SHANG-LIN PARK (detail) ca. 1st century A.D.

67 Attributed to **Yen Li-pên** THE THIRTEEN EMPERORS (detail: Hsüan-ti of the Ch'ên dynasty) 7th century

隋文帝楊堅在位廿
三至二五帝共世六年

68 Attributed to **Yen Li-pên** THE THIRTEEN EMPERORS (detail: Wên-ti of the Sui dynasty) 7th century

陳文帝在位八
年深崇道教

69 Attributed to **Yen Li-pèn**   THE THIRTEEN EMPERORS (detail: Wên-ti of the Ch'ên dynasty)   7th century

70 Emperor Hui-tsung THE FIVE-COLORED PARAKEET early 12th century

71 Emperor Hui-tsung LADIES PREPARING NEWLY WOVEN SILK (detail) early 12th century

72   **Emperor Hui-tsung**   Ladies Preparing Newly Woven Silk (detail)   early 12th century

73 Ch'ên Yung-chih

BUDDHA UNDER THE MANGO TREE   ca. A.D. 1025

74 Attributed to **Yen Li-pèn** SCHOLARS OF THE NORTHERN CH'I COLLATING THE CLASSICS (detail) ca. 11th century

75 WÊN-CHI'S RETURN TO CHINA (detail) 12th century

76 **Chao Po-chü** ᴇɴᴛʀʏ ᴏꜰ Hᴀɴ Kᴀᴏ-ᴛꜱᴜ ɪɴᴛᴏ Kᴜᴀɴ-ᴄʜᴜɴɢ (detail)　12th century

77 **Chou Chi-ch'ang** Arhats Bestowing Alms upon Beggars (detail) A.D. 1184

78 **Ch'ên Jung** THE NINE DRAGONS (detail) A.D. 1244

79 Attributed to **Tung Yüan** Clear Weather in the Valley (detail) 12th–13th century

80 Ma Yüan BARE WILLOWS AND DISTANT MOUNTAINS ca. 1200

81 Wang Yüan-ch'i SPRING MORNING AT YEN-T'AN (detail) A.D. 1711

82 Jar with Cover 5th–3rd century B.C.   **83** Ewer ca. 11th century

84 JAR (Wan-nien-hu)   7th–8th century

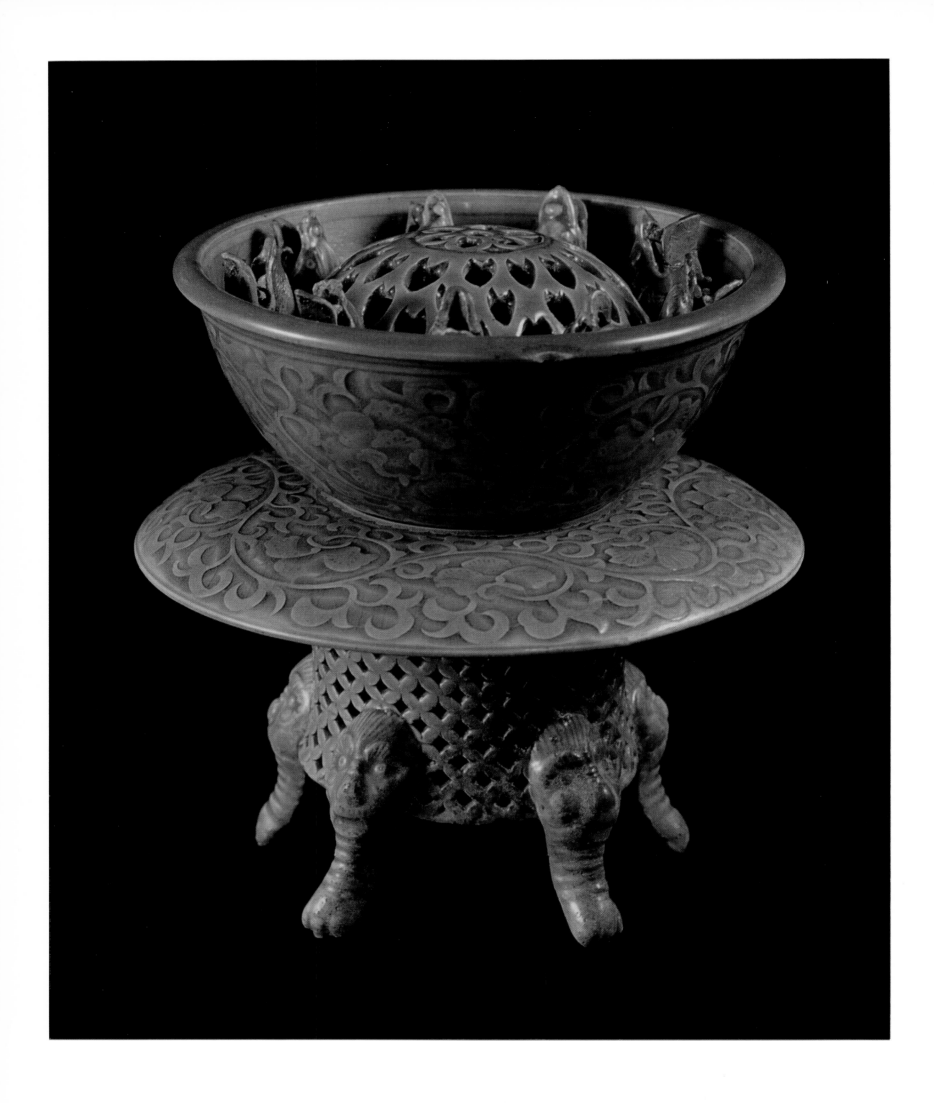

85 Ceremonial Bowl and Stand   ca. 11th century

86 Wine Bottle Tz'ŭ-chou 11th–12th century

87 VASE Tz'ŭ-chou 11th–12th century

88 COVERED VASE second half of the 14th century

89 VASE Koryŏ 11th–12th century

90   VASE   Koryŏ   12th century

91 CROWN 10th–11th century 92 EWER AND BASIN 11th–12th century

93 ALTARPIECE WITH AMITĀBHA AND ATTENDANTS   A.D. 593

94 LION   late 7th century

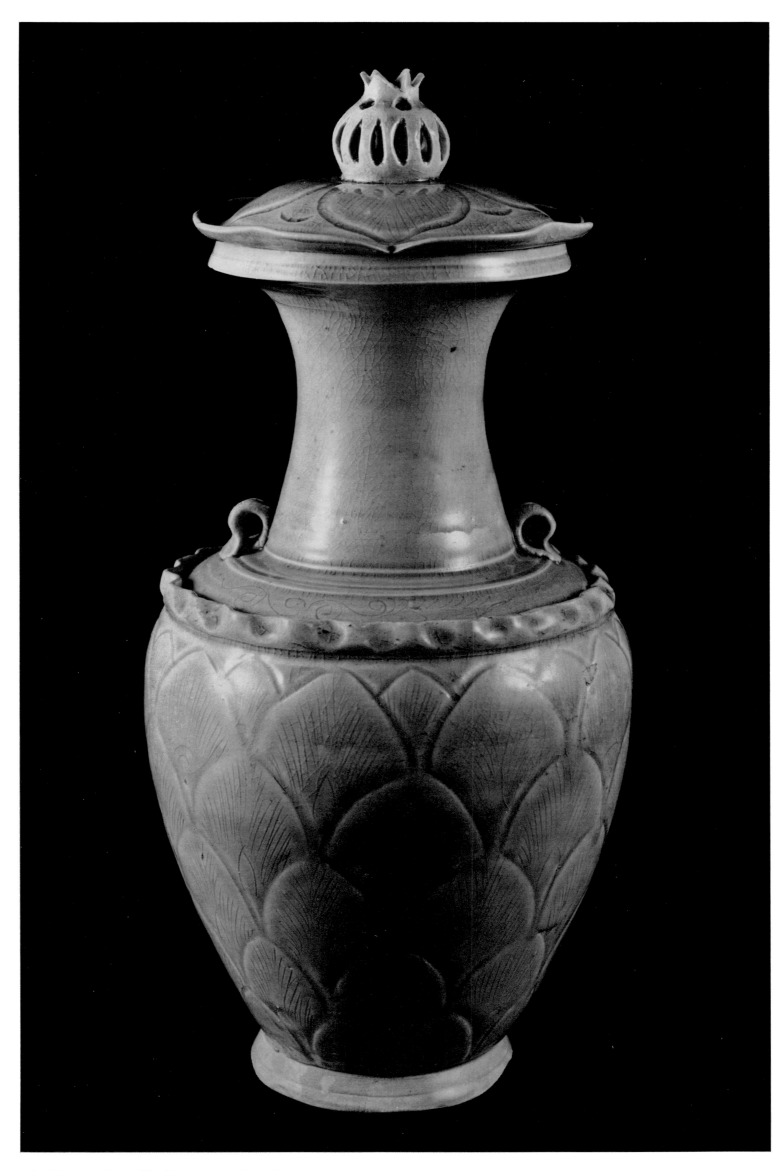

95 COVERED JAR   Yüeh ware   10th–11th century

96 Chao Ling-jang SUMMER MIST ALONG THE LAKE SHORE (detail) A.D. 1100

97 Wang Chên-p'êng MAHÂPRAJÂPATÎ HOLDING THE INFANT BUDDHA first half of the 14th century

98–99 Attributed to **Sung Kao-tsung** and **Ma Ho-chih** Six Odes of the Mao-shih (details) 12th century

100 Chu Ta
LOTUS IN THE MANNER OF HSÜ WEI
17th century

III Indian and Persian Art

101 YAKṢĪ ca. 25 B.C.

102 RAILING PILLAR WITH TWO FIGURES 2nd century A.D.

103 AVALOKITEŚVARA 6th century

104 DANCING APSARAS 11th century

105 Amitābha with Acolytes 12th–13th century

106 DARBAR OF JAHANGIR ca. A.D. 1620

107 Poet in a Garden   ca. a.d. 1610   **108** Śaṭha Nāyaka or the False Gallant   ca. a.d. 1690

109 K̥r̥ṣṇa and Rādhā Sheltering from the Rain   late 18th century

111   **Arraji Muhammad al Qawan**   A Triumphant Entry, from a manuscript of the Shāhnāma   A.D. 1552–1585

الحمد لله الذي أنزل على عبده الكتاب

والصلوة والسلام على محمد وآله وأصحابه خير الأنام

إن كتاب كرام واجب الإحترام كه هر مطلعي

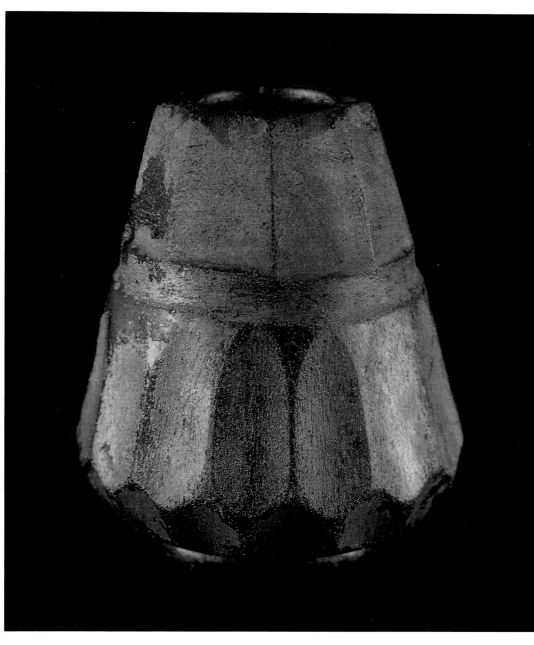

113 Bull's Head   12th century   **114** Statuette of a Man   12th century   **115** Vase   10th–12th century

116 Bowl Nishapur 10th century

117 BOWL Kashan early 13th century

118 Candelabrum mid 14th century

119 THE BODHISATTVA'S BATH IN THE NIRAÑJANA RIVER (detail)   1st century A.D.

121　Gautama Buddha　6th century

122 BUDDHA WITH TWO ATTENDANT BODHISATTVAS 8th century

123 Durgā as the Slayer of
the Buffalo Demon
8th century

124 VIŚVARŪPA VIṢṆU 9th century

125 ŚĀNTINĀTHA 10th century

126　Mahāvīra　10th–11th century

127　Lokanātha　11th century

128 MODEL CART WITH TWO BULLOCKS 2nd millenium B.C.

129 Hawk Attacking a Duck 10th–11th century

130 ELEPHANT 12th century

131 BOWL Minai ware late 12th–early 13th century

132 Ewer   early 15th century

خُذْ آنِاً فَصُبَّ فِيهِ خَلًّا حَامِضًا ثُمَّ عَلِّقِ الرَّصَاصَ فِيهِ وَلَا

يَلْصَقْ بِالْخَلِّ ثُمَّ طَيِّنْ فَمَ الْإِنَاءِ وَقِرَّهُ أَيَّامًا ثُمَّ افْتَحْهُ فَإِنْ كَانَ فِيهِ

صَلَاةُ الْإِسْفِنَاخ

اسْتِرْخَاءٌ فَاجْرُدْهُ ثُمَّ رَاعِهِ حَتَّى لَا يَبْقَى مِنْهُ شَيْءٌ وَإِذَا أَرَدْتَ

جَعْلَهُ أَقْرَاصَةً فَاعْجِنْهُ بِخَلٍّ حَامِضٍ ثُمَّ يَبِّسْهُ فِي الشَّمْسِ الْحَارِّ

فَإِنَّهُ يَكُونُ أَبْيَضَ بَالِغًا وَحَرَقُهُ إِنْ أَخَذْتَ جُزْءًا جَيِّدَكَ فَدَقَّهُ

وَنَفَرِّشُهُ عَلَيْهَا فِي بُرْمَةٍ وَهِيَ عَلَى جَمْرٍ ثُمَّ حَرِّكْهُ فَإِذَا أَتَى لَوْنُهُ

مِثْلَ الرَّمَادِ فَارْفَعْهُ وَبَرِّدْهُ وَهُوَ يُغْسَلُ مِثْلَ غَسْلِ الْقَدِيمِيَةِ طَبِيعَتُهُ

بَارِدَةٌ مُوَافِقٌ لِلْعِصَارَاتِ بِأَدِلَّةِ اللَّحْمِ الْمُنْتِنِ خَلْطِ الشَّمْعِ وَالْأَدْهَانِ

134 Vɪʙʜāsᴀ Rāɢɪṇī   ca. ᴀ.ᴅ. 1640

Catalogue

1

GIGAKU MASK
Japan, Heian period, ca. 11th century
Polychromed wood. H. 26.4 cm.
William Sturgis Bigelow Collection. 11.5940

This finely carved mask is an outstanding example of early Japanese woodcarving. Originally it must have been painted in bright colors and fitted with heavy eyebrows and a beard. The animated expression of the face with its protruding tongue is very similar to that of the so-called *Ni no mai* masks of the Bugaku dances. As is the case with the *Ni no mai* masks, the specific context in which this mask was used is not clear.

In the illustrated catalogue *Shūko Jūshū*, which appeared in 1800, Matsudaira Sadanobu (1758–1829) published drawings of thirty-eight Gigaku masks in the collection of the Tōdaiji temple in Nara. Of these masks nineteen are still in the collection of this temple. One of the drawings shows a mask which is almost identical in shape and size to the Boston piece. The indications of color given on the drawing correspond to the faded colors on our piece. In all likelihood the two pieces are identical.

2

ŚĀKYAMUNI
Japan, Heian Period, late 10th century
Katsura wood with gold and traces of polychromy.
H. 85.5 cm.
Gift of Denman Waldo Ross. 09.72

This solid wooden statue (Japanese: *ichiboku*) is carved from the wood of the Katsura tree (Cercidiphyllum Japonicum). The folds of the drapery resemble those of some dated statues of the end of the tenth century, especially the Yakushi (Bhaiṣajyaguru) image in Zensuiji temple in Shiga prefecture which bears a date corresponding to A.D. 993 (see *Zōzō meiki*, Tokyo, 1967, Vol. 1, no. 9).

The absence of a container for medicine or of any trace that such an attribute of Yakushi was ever attached to the palm of the left hand suggests that this statue is more likely to be a representation of the Historical Buddha than of the Healing Buddha Bhaiṣajyaguru.

3

DAI-ITOKU MYŌ-Ō
Japan, Heian period, 10th–11th century
Painted wood. H. 95 cm.
Special Japanese Fund. 05.228

This refined, superbly conceived image of Dai-itoku Myō-ō has lost little of its original artistic impact, even though it is

now in a rather fragmentary state of preservation. The top of the knot of hair on the head has been partially restored. Although it is not known whether the remarkably well preserved colors are original, it is unlikely that they are later than the Kamakura period.

Technically speaking, the statue represents a transitional stage from the one-block *(ichiboku)* technique to the joint-block *(yosegi)* technique. It conveys in a most convincing manner the new and more humane approach to Esoteric Buddhism which characterizes the spirit of the period during which it was carved.

Published: M. Anesaki, *Buddhist Art*, Boston and New York, 1915, Pl. XVII; Robert T. Paine and Alexander Soper, *The Art and Architecture of Japan*, Harmondsworth, 1955, Pl. 34b.

4

SHŌ KANNON (AVALOKITEŚVARA)
Japan, late Nara or early Heian period, late 8th–early 9th century
Hinoki wood. H. 178 cm.
Special Japanese Fund. 12.128

This figure of Avalokiteśvara is a splendid example of the monumental sculptural style of the end of the Nara period and the early years of the Heian period, and no comparable example exists in collections outside Japan. With the exception of the arms, part of the nose, and certain details of the drapery which are later restorations, the image is remarkably well preserved.

Okakura Kakuzō acquired this piece of sculpture for the Museum during a trip to Nara in 1911. Although its original provenance is unclear, there can be little doubt that it came from the Nara area, for there is a close stylistic resemblance to two groups of wooden statues, in the Tōshōdaiji and in the Daianji, both at Nara.

These two sets of figures of almost exactly the same size show the same folds of the drapery, resembling those of the dry lacquer statues of the Nara period, the same arrangement of the hairdress and a similar shape of face and eyebrows as this piece. However, the Boston statue is the only one of this type which represents Avalokiteśvara in a kind of *tribhanga* pose. It softens the somewhat ponderous and rigid effect which characterizes the other statues of this type and in this respect comes closer to the famous Eleven-headed Avalokiteśvara of the Hokkeji nunnery, also at Nara. The use of this classical Indian pose exemplifies the new influx of artistic ideas from the Asian continent with which the rise of the monumental Nara school of sculpture is often associated.

Published: M. Anesaki, *Buddhist Art*, Boston and New York, 1915, Pl. XIX; Robert T. Paine and Alexander Soper,

The Art and Architecture of Japan, Harmondsworth, 1955, Pl. 21b.

5
Saichi
SHŌ KANNON (AVALOKITEŚVARA)
Japan, Kamakura period, A.D. 1270
Bronze. H. 106.5 cm., D. (of base) 51 cm.
William Sturgis Bigelow Collection. 11.11447

This perfectly preserved masterpiece of Japanese bronze casting is a composite figure, consisting of several detachable parts. The seated Kannon is shown holding a lotus in the left hand; the right hand is in *vitarkamudrā*, the pose symbolizing argumentation. The elaborate halo is executed in an openwork floral (*hōsōge*) design; attached to it are disks bearing bīja graphs, Sanskrit letters which stand for figures of the Buddhist pantheon. The graph *sa*, symbolizing Kannon, has been repeated five times on both sides. The *a*-graph at the top symbolizes Dainichi Nyorai.

On the hexagonal base of the elaborate lotus throne is an engraved dedicatory inscription. From this inscription we know that the sculpture was cast in A.D. 1270, that the name of the artist is Saichi, and that the sculpture was originally in the temple Matsuodera in the village Hatagawa in Shiga prefecture. This temple is now known under the name of Kongōrinji.

Published: Yukio Yashiro, "Bosuton Bijutsukan shozō no meiki aru Nihon chōkoku" ("Inscribed Japanese Sculptures in the Boston Museum"), *Bijutsu Kenkyu*, no. 57, pp. 9–15.

6
Kaikei
MIROKU BOSATSU
Japan, Kamakura period, A.D. 1189
Wood, partially covered with gold lacquer. H. 107 cm.
Chinese and Japanese Special Fund. 20.723

This superb specimen of twelfth century Japanese sculpture in joint-block (*yosegi*) technique originally came from the Kōfukuji at Nara. It represents the Bodhisattva Miroku (Sanskrit: Maitreya), the Buddha of the Future. It was given to Okakura Kakuzō in 1903–1904. Five years later, when the statue had to be repaired because its head had become loose, a sūtra scroll was discovered inside. A colophon added to this scroll mentions as a date the fifth year of Bunji (A.D. 1189) and the name of the sculptor Kaikei. It is the earliest known dated work by this celebrated Buddhist monk-sculptor.

This sculpture and the painting representing Dai-itoku Myō-ō (see Pl. 10), both from the collection of Okakura Kakuzō, are among the greatest masterpieces of Japanese Buddhist art in the Museum of Fine Arts.

Published: Yukio Yashiro, "Bosuton Bijutsukan shozō no meiki aru Nihon chōkoku" ("Inscribed Japanese Sculptures in the Boston Museum"), *Bijutsu Kenkyu*, no. 57, pp. 9–15.

7
Kōshun
SŌGYŌ HACHIMAN
Japan, Kamakura period, A.D. 1328
Wood; crystal eyes. H. 82 cm.
Maria Antoinette Evans Fund and contribution. 36.413

Sōgyō Hachiman, the Shintō deity Hachiman in the guise of a Buddhist priest, is a figure associated with syncretic Shintō, a religious development in which Japan's native Shintō gods came to be regarded as manifestations of figures from the Buddhist pantheon.

This fine sculpture, executed in the joint-block (*yosegi*) technique, carries an inscription inside the head. The inscription indicates that the sculpture was carved by the sculptor Kōshun, a monk-sculptor of the rank of Hōgen at the Kōfukuji, Nara. Little is known about his life, but dated sculptures by him range from A.D. 1311 to 1569. Although the sculptor made an error when he recorded the name of the era (writing Jureki instead of Kareki), there can be no doubt that the sculpture was carved in the third year of Kareki, i.e., A.D. 1328.

Published: Kojiro Tomita, "Statue of Sōgyō Hachiman by Kōshun," *MFA Bulletin*, XXXV, 212 (1937), 78–81; Takeshi Kobayashi, "Bosuton Bijutsukan no Sōgyōzō ni tsuite" ("On a Statue of Sōgyō in the Boston Museum"), *Gasetsu*, III, 11 (1939), 100 ff.

8
HOKKEDŌ KOMPON MANDARA
Japan, Nara or early Heian period, late 8th–early 9th century
Ink and colors on hemp cloth. H. 107.4 cm., W. 144.3 cm.
William Sturgis Bigelow Collection. 11.6120

The painting represents the Buddha Śākyamuni expounding the Lotus Sūtra (Sanskrit: *Saddharmapuṇḍarīka sūtra*) to a host of heavenly and human beings who are assembled on top of Mount Gridhrakūṭa. The present name of the painting is derived from an inscription on the back which records its restoration in the fourth year of Kyū-an, i.e., A.D. 1148, by the celebrated monk-painter Chingai (1091–1152). That the painting was indeed originally included among the treasures of the Hokkedō of the temple Tōdaiji, Nara, is confirmed by a document in the temple records. It lists all works of art which were put on temporary display at the temple in 1726 and actually mentions this work. In 1884 it was acquired by William Sturgis Bigelow, who later gave it to the Museum.

In spite of the fact that the painting has been frequently retouched and that all of the figures in the foreground, the canopy of the Buddha, and the buildings in the background are restored—most probably by Chingai—it is still a work of art of great interest and importance, the one work among the few surviving paintings of the Nara period ever to leave Japan. The landscape in the background has lost most of its colors, revealing the ink painting underneath. The international character of the style of the landscape painting has created considerable confusion as to the original provenance of the work. The inscription on the back calls it Indian; Okakura considered it Chinese. In recent years, however, it has been generally accepted as a Japanese work of art of the Nara period.

Published: Takaaki Matsushita, "The Hokkedō Kompon Mandara," *Bijutsu Kenkyu*, no. 186 (1956), pp. 1 ff.; Yukio Yashiro, "The Hokkedō Kompon Mandara," *Bijutsu Kenkyu*, no. 192 (1957), pp. 1 ff.

9

FUGEN EMMEI

Japan, Heian period, mid 12th century
Ink, colors, and gold on silk. H. 141.5 cm., W. 88.5 cm.
Fenollosa-Weld Collection. 11.4036

The Bodhisattva Fugen Emmei (Sanskrit: Vajrāmoghasa-mayasattva), an esoteric form of Samantabhadra, is represented in strict accordance with a dhāranī-sūtra which was translated into Chinese by the famous monk Amoghavajra (705–774). (See *Taishō Daizōkyō*, no. 1136.) Fugen is shown holding a *vajra* and a bell. He is seated on a lotus throne on his mount, the three-headed elephant. The elephant is standing on the Wheel of Law, which in turn rests upon eight smaller elephants. Ranged on either side of the main figure stand the Four Guardian Kings. The iconography of the central figure is very similar to that of the Fugen Emmei of the temple Matsuno-o-dera in Kyoto. Both date from about the middle of the twelfth century.

This masterpiece of Japanese Buddhist painting is part of the collection assembled by Ernest F. Fenollosa in Japan between 1880 and 1886. The entire collection was bought by Charles G. Weld in 1886, and later bequeathed to the Boston Museum.

Published: M. Anesaki, *Buddhist Art*, Boston and New York, 1915, Pl. XXVI; Takashi Hamada, "Amerika ni okeru Heian Kaiga" ("Heian Painting in America"), *Bunkazai*, 1968, no. 4, pp. 22 ff.

10

DAI-ITOKU MYŌ-Ō

Japan, Heian period, 11th century
Ink, colors, and kirigane on silk. H. 192 cm., W. 118 cm.
Gift of William Sturgis Bigelow in Memory of Okakura Kakuzō. 20.750

This dramatic rendering of the six-armed, six-legged Dai-itoku Myō-ō (Sanskrit: Yamāntaka) shows this important figure of the esoteric Buddhist pantheon in all his awesome power and glory. The contrast of the strong, bold outlines with the delicate details of the attributes and cloth patterns, the bright, sparkling colors and the lively rendering of the flames surrounding the seated figure are typical for Japanese Buddhist painting of the eleventh century.

This masterpiece, perhaps the finest Buddhist painting ever to leave Japan, is one of the great discoveries of Okakura Kakuzō, who acquired it just before he resigned in 1898 as a curator of the Imperial Museum, Tokyo. During all the years of Okakura's travels and his stay in Boston, it remained in storage in his house in Japan, to be exhibited only once in the Kyoto Museum shortly after his death. Four years after the Memorial Exhibition in 1916 it was acquired by the Museum of Fine Arts. There are very few paintings of this size and importance of which the original provenance cannot be established; however, as the story of its provenance from the Daigoji in Kyoto has been disproved, the ultimate origin of this Dai-itoku Myō-ō remains shrouded in mystery.

Published: Yukio Yashiro, "Beikoku ni okeru ni dai butsuga" ("Two Great Buddhist Paintings in America"), *Bijutsu Kenkyu*, no. LXI (1937), pp. 1–10; Julia Meech, "A Painting of Daiitoku from the Bigelow Collection," *MFA Bulletin*, LXVII, 347 (1969), 18–43.

11

BATŌ KANNON

Japan, Heian period, 12th century
Ink, colors, and gold on silk. H. 165.5 cm., W. 83 cm.
Fenollosa-Weld Collection. 11.4035

Batō Kannon (Sanskrit: Hayagrīva), represented here with three heads and eight arms, is seated on an elaborately decorated lotus throne against a halo of golden hōsōge flowers. Although the figure has been given the dark red color and the horse's head in the headdress which iconographic texts describe, none of the existing texts give exactly the same combination of hands and attributes shown here.

There is a striking similarity between this painting and the famous Śākyamuni of the Jingoji at Kyoto. Not only are the thrones on the two paintings virtually identical, but most of the decorative patterns are also very similar. Even the width of the central strip of silk used for the painting is exactly the same. It is therefore more than likely that both paintings not only date from the same period, but were probably even painted at the same studio.

The provenance of this Batō Kannon was unknown until recently the label of the original mounting, removed many years ago, was rediscovered. It reads: "Treasure of the Kōshōji". The numerous temples of this name in Japan belong mostly to branches of the Zen sect, and it is therefore rather unlikely that the label states the ultimate origin of the icon.

Published: Robert T. Paine, *Ten Japanese Paintings,* New York, 1939, pp. 11–14; *Kokka,* no. 877.

12

DAINICHI AS ICHIJIKINRIN
Japan, Heian period, late 12th century
Ink and colors on silk. H. 125 cm., W. 79.5 cm.
Gift of Denman Waldo Ross. 09.387

Dainichi as Ichijikinrin (Sanskrit: Ekākṣara-uṣṇīṣacakra) is seated cross-legged in diamond pose on a white lotus, forming with his hands the *chiken-in* or wisdom fist. Flanked by four flower vases and with the Five Buddhas in his headdress, this representation of Mahāvairocana as the Lord of the Vajradhātu is in strict accordance with the iconographic regulations for Vajradhātu mandalas. Several closely related paintings of this type exist, including another, slightly later, example also in the Museum of Fine Arts.

The painting, partly colored from the back *(urasaishiki),* has lost some of its original coloring and several details have become blurred. A notice of its repair and remounting, dating from 1907, is signed by the abbot Takushō (1833–1915) of the Jingoji monastery near Kyoto. Shortly after its repair it was sold to Dr. Ross, who presented it to the Museum.

Published: John Rosenfield, *Japanese Arts of the Heian Period,* New York, 1967, no. 9.

13

NYO-IRIN KANNON
Japan, early Kamakura period, ca. 1200
Ink, colors, and gold on silk. H. 98.5 cm., W. 44.8 cm.
Fenollosa-Weld Collection. 11.4032

The six-armed Nyo-irin Kannon (Sanskrit: Cintāmaṇicakra) is represented in the attitude of royal ease on Mount Potalaka, the legendary abode of Avalokiteśvara which is known for its many waterfalls. Although the richly adorned golden figure is painted in strict accordance with the iconographic rules, the addition of three attendants in the lower

right corner is somewhat unusual. Basu Sennin (Sanskrit: Ṛṣi Vasu), Kichijōten (Sanskrit: Mahāśrī), and Zennishi Dōji (Sanskrit: Janavasabha) are more often associated with the thousand-armed Avalokiteśvara and Vaiśravaṇa (Bishamonten [see Pl. 14]) than with Cintāmaṇicakra.

It is difficult to give an exact date for this painting; some scholars having assigned it to the late Heian period; others have attributed it to the early Kamakura period. Stylistic affinities with works dating from around 1200 suggest a date in that period. It is probably slightly earlier than a similar painting in the Freer Gallery of Art, Washington, D.C.

Published: Takashi Hamada, "Amerika ni okeru Heian kaiga" ("Heian Painting in America"), *Bunkazai,* 1968, no. 4, pp. 22 ff.

14

BISHAMONTEN MANDARA
Japan, Kamakura period, late 12th–early 13th century
Ink, colors, and gold on silk. H. 119 cm., W. 68 cm.
Chinese and Japanese Special Fund. 05.202

Of all existing representations of Bishamonten (Sanskrit: Vaiśravaṇa) this mandala is one of the most complex, combining iconographic features of different types of representations of Bishamonten into one lively and colorful scene. It is only in the compendium of iconographic drawings by Shingaku (1117–1180), the famous *Besson zakki* (no. 289), that we find the Guardian King of the North surrounded by a larger retinue.

Supported by the triad made up of the Earth Goddess, Niramba, and Biramba, Vaiśravaṇa stands surrounded by his relatives and attendants. To his right we see Kichijōten and Zennishi dōji (see Pl. 10). The four-armed figure in the background can be identified as Karuratenshi, a rare figure of minor importance in the Buddhist pantheon, who also appears in iconographic drawings as an attendant of Vaiśravaṇa. Five Yakṣas stand to the left of Bishamonten; they are accompanied by two Rākṣasas in the foreground.

The artist, a superbly skilled draftsman, has rendered the profusion of iconographic details in a most meticulous and orderly, yet also imaginative and lively way. Although attributed by some to the late Heian period, certain stylistic features of this masterpiece of Japanese Buddhist painting would seem to fit best among the works of the first years of the Kamakura period. It was acquired for the Museum by Okakura Kakuzō and is said to have come from the Enryakuji on Mt. Hieizan.

Published: Takashi Hamada, "Amerika ni okeru Heian Kaiga" ("Heian Painting in America"), *Bunkazai,* 1968, no. 4, pp. 22 ff.

15–17
KIBI DAIJIN NITTŌ E-KOTOBA
Japan, Heian period, late 12th century
Ink and colors on paper. Handscroll, H. 32.2 cm., L. 2442 cm.
William Sturgis Bigelow Collection by exchange. 32.131

This famous handscroll illustrates the legendary adventures
of the Ambassador to the Chinese Court, Kibi no Makibi,
during his mission to T'ang China in 753. Aided by the
ghost of the celebrated poet, Abe no Nakamaro, the skillful
magician Kibi successfully passes the rigorous tests of skill
and learning to which he is subjected by his haughty Chinese
hosts. The purely fictional story—Abe no Nakamaro was
still alive at the time of Kibi's mission—seems to be of the
engi type. In it the proclaimed descendants of Kibi no
Makibi saw a support for their claim of supremacy over the
descendants of Abe no Nakamaro in the field of On'yōdō, a
generic term for various magical and pseudo-scientific
practices of Chinese origin. During the Heian period both
families regarded these practices as their specialty.

Executed in bright colors with great skill and an exquisite
sense of humor, this scroll is one of the finest examples of
Yamato-e painting in the United States. Its departure from
Japan resulted in the first Japanese legislation making the
export of art objects subject to governmental approval. It
was recently divided into four parts in order to ensure its
preservation.

Published: Robert T. Paine, "The Scroll of Kibi's
Adventures in China," *MFA Bulletin*, XXXI, 185 (1933),
2–12; Jan Fontein, "Kibi's Adventures in China: Facts,
Fiction, and Their Meaning," *MFA Bulletin*, LXVI, 344
(1968), 49–68.

18–20
HEIJI MONOGATARI EMAKI (THE BURNING OF THE SANJŌ
PALACE)
Japan, Kamakura period, third quarter of the 13th century
Ink and colors on paper. Handscroll, H. 41.3 cm., L. 699.7 cm.
Fenollosa-Weld Collection. 11.4000

The wars between the Taira and Minamoto clans were an
episode in the eventful history of feudal Japan which
remained through the ages an inexhaustible source of
inspiration for the artists. The earliest, now extant, and also
one of the most impressive pictorial renderings of these
events is a series of handscrolls known as the Heiji Monogatari Emaki. Once a large series of handscrolls, it now
consists only of three scrolls and some scattered fragments.
The scroll depicting the night attack on the Sanjō Palace,
acquired in Japan by Ernest Fenollosa sometime before
1886, is the finest of the three scrolls.

In it the anonymous artist has illustrated the night attack

of January 19, 1160, on the Sanjō Palace by the combined
forces of Fujiwara Nobuyori and Minamoto Yoshitomo and
the subsequent abduction of the retired Emperor Go-
Shirakawa. The painting represents the culmination of a
technique for which the Yamato-e artists were famous: the
skillful handling of large crowds of people. The artist has
done justice to the individuality of each person; yet at the
same time he has managed to convey the nervous tension of
the battlefield by creating, out of the countless individual
persons, crowds which have an organic unity of their own,
moving towards the scene of the battle and regrouping
afterwards around the imperial carriage. Between these two
crowds lies the Palace, going up in flames, while the scene
dissolves into scattered hand to hand fights, full of the fierce
brutality which characterized these civil wars.

Published: Kojiro Tomita, "The Burning of the Sanjō
Palace," *MFA Bulletin*, XXII, 139 (1925), 50–55; Edwin O.
Reischauer, "The Hour of the Ox," *Horizon*, XI, 1 (1969),
12–25.

21–24
THE GAY QUARTERS OF KYOTO
Japan, Edo period, second half of the 17th century
Ink, colors, and gold on paper. Pair of six-fold screens,
H. 104.5 cm., W. 45.5 cm. (each panel)
Gift of Denman Waldo Ross. 06.286–287

In the manner which is characteristic of the genre painters
of the second half of the seventeenth century, the anonymous
artist has painted a vivid impression of the colorful life in
the gay quarters of Kyoto. One screen (Pls. 21 and 24) shows
a crowd of people strolling along a street lined with houses of
pleasure. The other screen (Pls. 22 and 23) shows a large tea
house with a garden full of people amusing themselves.

The two outside panels of this last screen were lost and
have been replaced by panels which carry specimens of the
handwriting of the priest Takasabu Ryūtatsu (died 1611).
The first of the forty-six poems, in the upper right corner,
is the *Kimigayo*, here written in exactly the same version as
that of the present national anthem of Japan. In the lower
left corner the last of the eight sheets carries the signature
of Ryūtatsu and the date Keichō seventh year, corresponding
to 1602.

Published: Muneshige Narasaki, *Shoki Ukiyo-e Kaisetsu*,
Tokyo, 1962, p. 53.

25–26
Ogata Kōrin (1658–1716)
MATSUSHIMA
Japan, Edo period, early 18th century

Ink and colors on paper. Six-fold screen, H. 155 cm., W. 63 cm. (each panel)
Fenollosa-Weld Collection. 11.4584

In this grandiose composition, which was obviously inspired by Sōtatsu's earlier rendering of the same theme (Freer Gallery of Art, Washington, D.C.), Kōrin has skillfully symbolized the scenery of the archipelago in the Bay of Matsushima, northeast of Sendai. The almost eight hundred islands constitute one of the three Famous Views of Japan. The pine-clad rocks of Matsushima, rising from the foaming waves, were an ideal theme for the masters of the Rimpa-school, who repeated it again and again in their works. The fact that Kōrin signs as *Hokkyō*, an honorary title he received in 1701 when he was forty-four years old, indicates that this screen, probably one of a pair, was painted after the turn of the century.

This screen is one of the first purchases of Ernest Fenollosa, made on his first trip to Kyoto in 1880. It is, in all probability, the first major work of Japanese art to be acquired by a foreigner.

Published: Ichimatsu Tanaka, ed., *The Art of Kōrin*, Tokyo, 1959, Pl. 23.

27–28
Sōtatsu School
POPPIES
Japan, Edo period, 17th century
Colors and gold on paper. Pair of six-fold screens, H. 149 cm., W. 56.5 cm. (each panel)
Gift of Mrs. W. Scott Fitz. 11.1272–1273

The artist has painted a garden of flowering poppies in bright colors against a wide expanse of gold. In the best tradition of the Sōtatsu school, this composition derives its decorative effect not from a bold display of calligraphy with strongly painted contours, but rather from simple, "bone-less" painting in thin, diaphanous colors which makes the gold ground shine through the green of the leaves.

The screens have no signature or seal. A label on the back of one of the screens attributed them to Sōtatsu and states that they were presented to the temple Tentoku-in at Kōyasan by the Lord Maeda. In 1623 an older temple was renamed Tentoku-in when the ashes of the wife of Maeda Toshitsune (1593–1658), who was the second daughter of Tokugawa Hidetada (1579–1632), were deposited there. This information is of special interest because it is known that Sōtatsu painted the sliding doors of the Yōgen-in in Kyoto, when this temple was reconstructed in 1621 at the request of Hidetada and his wife. Although the facts mentioned in the label may be correct, it should be pointed out

that the label cannot antedate the Meiji era as it refers to the Maeda family as holding the rank of marquis.

Published: Robert T. Paine, *Ten Japanese Paintings*, New York, 1939, pp. 47–50.

29
EUROPEAN KING AND COURTIERS
Japan, Edo period, early 17th century
Ink, colors, and gold on paper. Six-fold screen, H. 127 cm., W. 55.6 cm. (each panel)
Fenollosa-Weld Collection. 11.4312

This screen is a fine example of Japanese painting created under the influence of Portuguese Jesuit artists, several of whom came to Japan prior to the expulsion of the Portuguese and the suppression of Christianity in the early seventeenth century. The mixture of what must have been, in the eyes of the Japanese artists, strange and exotic elements, all derived from prints and paintings which missionaries had imported from Portugal, is too hybrid to allow us to establish the exact date or the identity of the prototypes.

The pigments have been thickened with a white body and glue in order to imitate the effect of opaque oil painting. This set shows a strong resemblance to works which bear the European style seal of an artist whose name was Nobukata, but about whose life nothing is known.

Published: Robert T. Paine, *Japanese Screen Paintings; Landscapes and Figures*, Boston, 1938, no. 4.

30
THE ARRIVAL OF A PORTUGUESE SHIP IN JAPAN
Japan, Edo period, early 17th century
Ink, colors, and gold on paper. Six-fold screen, H. 154.5 cm., W. 59.5 cm. (each panel)
Fenollosa-Weld Collection. 11.4168.

This screen is one of a well-known genre in which Japanese artists of the Kano school, following the vogue of the day, illustrated the arrival of the "Southern Barbarians" (Namban) in Japan. The left side of this screen is entirely taken up by a fanciful rendering of a Portuguese carrack from which merchandise is being unloaded into a boat. From the shore the "kapitan" watches the proceedings, escorted by a servant holding a payoong over his master's head; meanwhile the Japanese shopkeepers in the back-ground await the disembarkation of the foreign clientele. The foreigners' faces have been reduced to a uniform stereotype. Thus, there is little distinction between the Portuguese and the servants with their dark complexion, Indians from Goa and other settlements on the coast of India who had entered into the service of the Portuguese. The other screen of this pair represents a view of a Chinese harbor, a rather unusual theme in this genre.

Published: Tokutarō Nagami, *Namban Byōbu Taisei*, 1930, Pls. 98–99; Robert T. Paine, *Japanese Screen Paintings; Landscapes and Figures*, Boston, 1938, no. 5.

31–32
A VIEW OF SHIJŌ-KAWARAMACHI
Japan, Edo period, 17th century
Ink, colors, and gold on paper. Pair of six-fold screens, H. 104 cm., W. 49.5 cm. (each panel)
Fenollosa-Weld Collection. 11.4591–4592

On two six-fold screens, the anonymous artist has painted a panoramic view of the Shijō-Kawaramachi section of Kyoto, extending as far as the Kamo River. This section was the theater and amusement district of the ancient capital. One side of the street is lined with theaters which offer a great variety of diversions; on the other side, animal sideshows, jugglers and buffoons compete with each other for the favor of the public, while a tightrope walker performs high above the crowd. Actors perform on stage (Pl. 32) as well as in the street (Pl. 31). A *shamisen* player who is seated in a chair covered with a tiger skin (Pl. 32) also occurs on a screen in the Seikadō Foundation, Tokyo (see *Rakuchū Rakugaizu*, Kyoto, 1966, Pl. 24). On that screen there is a poster at the entrance of the theater which identifies the scene as *Sadojima Kabuki*, an early type of Kabuki, first performed by the Sadojima family in 1614.

The accurate and lively rendering of innumerable details makes this pair of screens a fascinating document for our knowledge of the Japanese theater and amusement world of the early Edo period.

Published: Takutarō Sakakura, *Nihon Bungaku Zu-e*, Kyoto, 1957, Pl. 246 above.

33
THEATER SCENES AT FUKIYA-CHŌ
Japan, Edo period, late 17th–early 18th century
Ink, colors, and gold on paper. Six-fold screen, H. 54 cm., W. 28.7 cm. (each panel)
Fenollosa-Weld Collection. 11.4623

This double-faced screen shows a theater scene on one side with a large group of actors on the stage and spectators. The entire scene is framed in clouds of gold. The opposite side shows the entrances to a row of theaters along the Fukiya-chō in the theater district of Edo. The theater on the right is that in which the scene on the other side of the screen is performed; thereby the logical connection between the two sides is established.

The artist has rendered the two scenes with painstaking attention to such details as the texts of the theater bills (*bangumi*) and the costumes of the actors. Of special interest is the view of the interior of the *jōruri* theater, the Iseno-daijō, which is shown on the left side, above the line of the roofs of the theaters. Although Wakatsuki has tried to establish 1674 or 1675 as the date of the painting on the basis of the posted programs of the theaters, the style of painting suggests a date of at least twenty-five years later.

Published: Yasuji Wakatsuki, *Kinsei Shoki Kokugeki no Kenkyū*, pp. 584–591.

34
Mori Sosen (1749–1821)
MONKEYS
Japan, Edo period, late 17th century
Ink and slight colors on paper. Pair of six-fold screens, H. 158.6 cm., W. 58.2 cm. (each panel)
William Sturgis Bigelow Collection. 11.8590–8591

Mori Sosen, the most famous of the Japanese painters who specialized in the painting of monkeys, treats his favorite subject with the intimate feeling and insight of one who has based his craft on the close observation of these animals in their natural surroundings. In this series of twelve paintings he shows his monkeys in a variety of poses and groupings against settings of different seasons. The screens are signed with the signature which the artist used until he was about sixty years old.

35–36
Kōrin School
SPRING AND AUTUMN FLOWERS
Japan, Edo period, first half of 18th century
Ink, colors, gold, and silver on paper. Set of four *fusuma* panels, H. 168.5 cm., W. 69 cm. (each panel)
Denman Waldo Ross Collection. 17.805–808

These sliding doors were once part of a lavishly decorated room, and represent the trend toward ostentation in decoration which developed during the eighteenth century. They bear no signature, and are somewhat sharper in delineation and harder in color scheme than the works of the Kōrin-Kōetsu tradition, to which they are obviously related.

Published: Robert T. Paine, *Japanese Screen Paintings; Birds, Flowers, and Animals*, Boston, 1935, Pl. 28.

37
Torii Kiyonaga (1752–1815)
A MOTHER AND DAUGHTER UNDER A WILLOW TREE
Japan, Edo period, late 18th century

Ink and colors on silk. H. 87.6 cm., W. 35 cm.
William Sturgis Bigelow Collection. 11.7531

The daughter, who is sitting on a bench, turns toward her mother who is standing next to her. The mother is dressed in a *kasuri* kimono, the daughter in a pale beige kimono. The mother and daughter theme occurs frequently in Kiyonaga's work. This painting is an example of his style around 1785. It is signed Seki Kiyonaga.

Between 1782 and 1787, Kiyonaga started to use his original family name, Seki, again as an indication of his wish to make himself independent from the Torii traditions and to establish his own artistic style.

38
ATSUITA KARAORI
Japan, Edo period, late 18th century
Twill and satin weave *(karaori)*. H. 145 cm.
Gift of William Sturgis Bigelow. 15.1157

Karaori or "Chinese weave" is a rich type of brocade, originally imported from China and later also woven in Japan, which is characterized by colorful designs in satin weave on a twill ground. In later times the name came to be applied to Nō costumes woven in this technique. These colorful garments were used only for women's roles in Nō plays, but a slightly different type, known as *atsuita karaori*, were also used for men's roles. One of the characteristics of *atsuita karaori* is the lattice pattern in the decoration. Here a green and red, diamond-shape lattice pattern forms the background for colorful combinations of five-petaled flowers. The costume is a typical example of the rich and colorful style of the Nō garment which became common during the later part of the Edo period.

39
VASE
Japan, Kamakura period, 14th century
Ko-Seto ware. H. 25 cm., D. 17.8 cm.
Gift of Miss Theodora Lyman. 19.880

This vase is a fine example of Ko-Seto ware of the Kamakura period. The impressed design of chrysanthemum scrolls is covered with a thin, crackled yellowish glaze. This vase was given to the Museum on loan in 1915; at that time it was described as a Chinese piece.

40
DISH
Japan, Edo period, early 17th century
Shino ware, inlaid decoration. H. 7 cm., L. 28 cm.
Charles B. Hoyt Collection. 50.1698

This three-legged, deep Shino ware dish with a gray, so-called "mouse colored" glaze (Japanese: *Nezumi Shino*) has an incised decoration, filled in with white slip, consisting of a flowering shrub. Within the frame of a border decorated with lines and spirals the artist has drawn a delicate and elegant design of vines and leaves.

The dish is a typical example of early Shino ware and bears a strong resemblance to pieces excavated from kiln sites in the vicinity of Kujiri, Mino.

Published: Arakawa Toyozō, *Shino*, *Tōji Zenshū*, Tokyo, 1959, vol. 4, fig. 49.

41
DISH
Japan, Edo period, late 17th century
Ko-Kutani porcelain. D. 34.7 cm.
Edward S. Morse Memorial Fund. 34.78

The dish is decorated with a landscape within an octagonal double frame, surrounded by eight medallions against a background of swastika patterns. The decoration is executed in green, yellow, blue, red, black, and aubergine enamels; a color scheme which is typical of the early products of the Kutani kilns.

42
JAR
Japan, Edo period, late 17th century
Kakiëmon porcelain, enameled decoration. H. 20.2 cm., D. 16.5 cm.
Edward S. Morse Memorial Fund. 57.383

This porcelain jar with flat shoulder, short neck, and wide mouth is decorated with chrysanthemums and rocks in red, yellow, blue, and green enamels. The vertical zig-zag design on the neck and the petal rays around the shoulder are often found on the wares of the early Kakiëmon potters. The dull, cream colored, crackled ground occurs on several other pieces of this type. The jar is generally attributed to one of the first three Kakiëmon masters, but the identification of their wares is still largely a matter of speculation.

43
TEBAKO (HANDY BOX)
Japan, Kamakura period, 14th century
Gold lacquer. H. 15.5 cm., W. 23.5 cm., L. 31 cm.
Martha Silsbee Fund. 31.1

The box, which has pewter rims and which is fitted with two brass ornaments in the shape of butterflies, is decorated with a variety of floral designs.

On the cover there is a weeping willow and a flowering

plum tree with flying birds around it. The sides of the box are decorated with a design of autumnal flowers, which are executed in *togidashi* (polished lacquer) and in *taka-makie* (raised gold lacquer).

Three rocks in the foreground of the trees on the cover have been inlaid with graphs reading *Chō sei den*. The Ch'ang-shêng-tien (Japanese: Chōseiden), the Hall of Longevity, was a palace hall built for the T'ang Emperor, Hsüan-tsung. Here, the term refers to a congratulatory poem in the *Wakan Ro-eishū*, written by the Japanese poet Yoshishige no Yasutane (late tenth century). The graphs on the rocks, and the spring and autumn scenes on the cover and box all refer to this poem: "In the Hall of Longevity, Springs and Autumns are abundant; in front of the Gate of Never-aging, the Sun and Moon move slowly." This auspicious theme is the motif on several lacquer boxes of the late Kamakura period. This box came originally from the collection of Kawasaki Yoshitarō.

Published: Kojiro Tomita, "A Japanese Lacquer Box of the Fourteenth Century," *MFA Bulletin*, XXIX, 25 (1931), 23–26.

44

Suzuribako (Ink Stone Box)
Japan, Edo period, 17th century
Lacquerwork. L. 22.1 cm., W. 24.2 cm.
William Sturgis Bigelow Collection. 11.10161

The box is covered with a design evoking the thought of autumn. The autumn flowers over a garden fence have been executed in lacquer relief *(takamakie)*, and mother-of-pearl on a black ground decorated with gold *(hirame)*. The box has been traditionally attributed to Igarashi Dōho (1643–1678), a distinguished lacquerworker from the Kaga province (Ishikawa prefecture). The combination of gold lacquer and mother-of-pearl in the decoration is typical of the work of this master and his family.

45

Ogawa Haritsu (1663–1747)
Box for Writing Paper
Japan, Edo period, 17th–18th century
Paulownia wood with inlaid decoration. H. 11.2 cm., L. 28.5 cm., W. 23.8 cm.
08.170

The paulownia wood surface has been covered by a thin layer of transparent lacquer. The elaborate inlaid design consists of palmetto leaves made of gold lacquer, mother-of-pearl, pottery, and lead, all in different colors.

Ogawa Haritsu, better known by the name Ritsu-ō, was

one of the first Japanese lacquermasters to fully exploit the decorative possibilities of inlaid designs executed in different materials of contrasting color. The box, a typical example of his work, carries the *kan* seal of the artist.

46

School of Geiami
Jittoku Laughing at the Moon
Japan, Ashikaga period, late 15th century
Ink on paper. H. 77.7 cm., W. 40 cm.
Fenollosa-Weld Collection. 11.4123

Kanzan and Jittoku, the two legendary Chinese Buddhist priests of the T'ang period, became a favorite subject of Japanese painters of the monochrome Zen school. One of the earliest Japanese representations is the Kanzan by the fourteenth century artist Kaō, a work now in the National Museum, Tokyo. Although no early example of a set of two paintings has survived, a comparison of the Kanzan by Kaō and this representation of Jittoku suggests that the poses of both figures, one bent forward, the other leaning backward, were created deliberately for compositional balance.

There is not sufficient evidence to support the tradition which attributes this painting of Jittoku to Geiami (1431–1485), but the brushwork has a close affinity to that of his school.

Published: M. Anesaki, *Buddhist Art*, Boston and New York, 1915, Pl. XL.

47

Bunsei (ca. mid 15th century)
Landscape
Japan, Ashikaga period
Ink and slight colors on paper. H. 73 cm., W. 33 cm.
Special Chinese and Japanese Fund. 05.203

In a masterful display of delicate brush technique, the artist has painted a landscape which, in spite of the many reminiscences of Southern Sung masters, is typically Japanese. This Japanese style of landscape painting originated in the early fifteenth century with such masters as the famous Josetsu. Traditional connoisseurs have always considered the *Bunsei* seal, which appears in the lower right corner of this painting, as one of Josetsu's seals. The Japanese art historian, Fukui Rikichirō, was the first to suggest that Bunsei was another artist, active at a slightly later time than Josetsu. A painting representing Vimalakīrti, now in the museum Yamato Bunkakan, Nara, bears the same seal and a date corresponding to A.D. 1457.

Okakura Kakuzō, who acquired this landscape for the Museum, assumed it to be identical with a work mentioned in the mid nineteenth century catalogue *Koga Bikō*. If that is correct, this landscape must have once belonged to the famous Tea Master, Kobori Enshū (1598–1647), even though it does not seem to be mentioned in the existing inventory of Enshū's possessions.

Published: Rikichirō Fukui, "A Landscape by Bunsei in the Boston Museum," *Burlington Magazine*, XLI, 236 (November 1922), 218–227; Robert T. Paine, *Ten Japanese Paintings*, New York, 1939, pp. 35–39.

48
Tan'an Chiden (late 15th–early 16th century)
NIGHT HERON
Japan, Ashikaga period
Ink on paper. H. 86.2 cm., W. 35.6 cm.
William Sturgis Bigelow Collection. 11.6335

Little is known about the life of the artist Tan'an Chiden. According to the *Tōhaku Gasetsu*, the "Talks on Painting" by the painter Hasegawa Tōhaku (1539–1610) (see Pl. 52) as told to the priest Nittsū of the Hompōji temple, Chiden was the son of an artisan of Amagasaki near Ōsaka. His father trained him to decorate articles of handicraft, which he did until the famous painter Sōami (died 1525) invited him to become his pupil. Chiden died at the early age of of twenty-five or twenty-six, which helps to explain why so few of his works have been preserved.

Two of his paintings (one in the National Museum, Tokyo, and this painting) represent *Goisagi*, a kind of Night Heron (Nycticorax Nycticorax). The two works are remarkably close in style, but the seals are slightly different (cf. *Bijutsu Kenkyu*, no. 16). Although the possibility should not be excluded that the seal on our painting was added later, it is probably identical with that on another work by Chiden (now in the Hosomi collection, Osaka) representing a bird on a branch.

The early monochrome artists often chose themes which could be given an appropriate Zen interpretation. The *Tōhaku Gasetsu* mentions a painting of a *Goisagi* by Mokuan (first half of the fourteenth century) which has an inscription reading "When the water becomes clear, fishes appear." Muddy water becoming clear could symbolize the disappearance of delusion; the speedy, unerring movement with which the bird catches his glittering prey could illustrate the experience of Sudden Enlightenment (Japanese: *satori*) which the Zen Buddhists sought to achieve.

Published: Takaaki Matsushita, *Suiboku Painting of the Muromachi Period*, Vol. I, Tokyo, 1960, Pl. 85.

49–50
Zōsan (early 16th century)
THE FOUR SEASONS
Japan, Ashikaga period
Ink, slight colors, and sprinkled gold on paper. Pair of six-fold screens, H. 158 cm., W. 56.6 (each panel)
Fenollosa-Weld Collection. 11.4149–4150

In strong and purposeful, sometimes almost harsh brush-strokes, the artist has painted a landscape which illustrates in one continuous composition the four seasons and their transitions.

Both screens bear the same two seals, one reading *Sōtan*, the other *Zōsan*. In an early catalogue of Japanese painting, the *Honchō Gashi*, first published in 1678, both seals are identified as those of the artist Oguri Sōtan, a painter about whom almost nothing is known. However, it would seem to be more likely that Sōtan and Zōsan were two different artists. A connoisseur, accepting the assumption of the *Honchō Gashi* as an established fact, may have added the Sōtan seal to these two screens. A slight difference in color between the two seals would seem to support this explanation.

Although nothing is known about the life of the artist Zōsan and only a few works by him have been preserved, the style of these landscape paintings suggests that he may have been active around the beginning of the sixteenth century.

Published: Takaaki Matsushita, *Suiboku Painting of the Muromachi Period*, Vol. I, Tokyo, 1960, Pl. 105.

51
Sesshū (1420–1506)
MONKEYS AND BIRDS IN TREES
Japan, Ashikaga period, 1491
Ink on paper. Six-fold screen (one of a pair), H. 160.6 cm., W. 61 cm. (each panel)
Fenollosa-Weld Collection. 11.4141

This screen, one of a pair which was acquired in Japan by Fenollosa from the collection of the Kishū Tokugawa family, is another example of the monochrome style of painting which developed in Japan under the influence of Chinese works of the Sung period. Sesshū's inspiration for this painting of monkeys, which is extremely attractive in spite of some overpainting and repairs, was undoubtedly Mu-ch'i's rendering of the same theme (in the Daitokuji, Kyoto). Although he was by no means the first master to adopt this popular subject of the Ch'an school, Sesshū was certainly one of the most successful artists in this genre.

In the upper right corner there is a signature which

reads: "Sesshū of Southern Bitchū made this in his seventy second summer." As this indicates his Japanese age (one year more than Western age) the painting must date from the year 1491. The signature closely resembles that on other works by the master and is accepted as authentic by most authorities.

Sesshū continued to paint brilliantly until he was well over eighty years old, and it is not surprising therefore that his work, painted at the age of seventy-one, shows no sign at all of a weakening of his artistic talents.

Published: Robert T. Paine, *Japanese Screen Paintings; Birds, Flowers, and Animals*, Boston, 1935, No. 1; Tokyo National Museum, ed. *Sesshū*, Tokyo, 1956, Pl. 29; *Tōkyō Kokuritsu Hakubutsukan Kiyō*, Tokyo, 1966, II, 87.

52
Hasegawa Tōhaku (1539–1610)
MONKEYS
Japan, Momoyama period, late 16th century
Ink on paper. Six-fold screen (one of a pair), H. 153.5 cm., W. 59.4 cm. (each panel)
William Sturgis Bigelow Collection. 11.7071

Hasegawa Tōhaku was one of the great artists of Japanese monochrome painting, but his genius has been recognized only in modern times. Like Sesshū (Pl. 51) he was strongly influenced by the works of the Chinese Ch'an masters, for whom he had a deep admiration, as is evident from his "Talks on Painting," the *Tōhaku Gasetsu* (see description, Pl. 48).

In spite of the fact that it carries the signature and seal of Sesson (neither of which is authentic), this pair of screens has long been attributed to Tōhaku, and is sometimes even thought to be part of the paintings remaining from the Ryōsen-an set of the Myōshinji temple, Kyoto. This set is known as "The monkeys with the cut arms" because Maeda Toshinaga (1562–1614) cut off some of the arms when he felt threatened by these monkeys during a nightmare (see *Kokka*, no. 337). However, all except two of these famous Tōhaku paintings seem to have been destroyed by fire. There are also slight discrepancies in the style of painting and in the size of the paper, but the correct evaluation of these differences is difficult because of the much poorer state of preservation of our paintings.

The present arrangement of the panels of the two screens, which was changed after the paintings came to Boston, is not entirely satisfactory, and it would seem that during much earlier attempts at restoration parts of the trees were added in order to make the reconstruction more convincing. Also, cleaning of the surface seems to have slightly blurred the hairy texture of the monkeys' fur, making it look different

from that of the monkeys on the screens in Myōshinji and the Shōkokuji (see *Kokka*, no. 900). However, even if it is unlikely that these screens should be part of the celebrated Myōshinji set, the attribution to Tōhaku would seem to be firmly established. In all probability they are somewhat earlier than Tōhaku's set of dragon and tiger screens, also in the Museum of Fine Arts, which bears a date corresponding to 1606.

Published: Robert T. Paine, *Japanese Screen Painting; Birds, Flowers, and Animals*, Boston, 1935, no. 9.

53
Keishoki (late 15th-early 16th century)
LANDSCAPE
Japan, Ashikaga period
Ink on paper. H. 39 cm., W. 91 cm.
Fenollosa-Weld Collection. 11.4127

This early Japanese landscape painting, now mounted as a kakemono, but probably originally part of a handscroll, is the work of Keishoki, a monk-painter of the Zen monastery Kenchōji at Kamakura. In keeping with the vogue of his time, Keishoki created a landscape, the configuration of which recalls a Yangtze River scene rather than any scenery in the artist's native country. The style is a crisp and sensitive rendition of the Southern Sung style of such masters as Hsia Kuei; but in spite of the fact that his source of inspiration is unmistakable, Keishoki has obviously developed a distinct personal style of his own.

The two seals in the lower corner reading *Kenkō* and *Shōkei* are the same as those which appear on Keishoki's masterpiece, a landscape in the Nezu Museum, Tokyo. Both paintings display the same brushwork and are very close to each other in style and quality. Although this painting was discovered in the collection in the course of a survey made by the Japanese art historian, Nakagawa Chūjun, in the spring of 1915, this masterpiece of early Japanese landscape painting is published here for the first time.

54
Kano Eitoku? (1543–1590)
TIGER
Japan, Momoyama period, 16th century
Ink on paper. Six-fold screen (one of a pair), H. 150.2 cm., W. 64 cm. (each panel)
Fenollosa-Weld Collection. 11.4446

This pair of screens, which are early works of the Kano school, are monochrome paintings in the Chinese tradition, inspired by the dragon and tiger paintings of the Southern Sung period. The other screen of this pair represents a dragon.

In the left corner is a round seal with a tripod inside reading *Kuninobu*. Some consider this unusual seal to be that of Kano Eitoku. Because the style of the painting seems slightly later than that of other works attributed to this master, the identification of the seal is not above question. In fact, this point was raised by the author of the *Koga Bikō* (ed. 1850). Even if some question remains as to the identity of its artist, there can be no doubt that these screens are very fine examples of the early Kano school.

Published: Robert T. Paine, *Japanese Screen Paintings; Birds, Flowers and Animals*, Boston, 1935, no. 7.

55
Tōyō (15th century)
THE THREE SAGES
Japan, Ashikaga period
Ink on paper. H. 33 cm., W. 46 cm.
Gift of Robert Treat Paine, Jr. 51.2490

This representation of the Three Sages; Buddha, Confucius, and Lao-tzŭ; now forms the central icon of a triptych, the other two paintings of which represent lotuses. The flowers are painted in the "boneless" manner, i.e. drawn without the use of linear contours, but the trinity of the Three Doctrines is drawn in softly flowing outlines. Whether the three paintings did originally belong together, and, if so, what the meaning of this unusual combination of themes could be, is not clear.

All three paintings carry the seal of *Tōyō*, an artist whose identity has been a matter of much discussion among Japanese art historians in recent years. Some believe that Tōyō is the name of the artist Sesshū (see Pl. 51), who may have used the name Sessō Tōyō prior to his voyage to China in 1468. Little is known about Sesshū's style of painting before he was exposed to Chinese artists and Chinese scenery, but the subtle effect of the use of ink gradations which this triptych displays is not typical of Sesshū's later works.

The triptych was originally preserved in the Bishamondō temple in Kyoto and was bought by Mr. Paine, then a young student living in Japan, at an auction of the treasures of this temple.

Published: S. Hasumi, *The Study of Sesshū Tōyō*, Tokyo, 1961, Pl. 3; Isamu Iijima, "Study of the Signatures and Seals of Sesshū Tōyō—in Connection with Sessō Tōyō," *Proceedings of the Tokyo National Museum*, Vol. 2, 1966.

56
Kano Tanyū (1602–1674)
CONFUCIUS AT THE APRICOT ALTAR
Japan, Edo period, 17th century
Ink and slight colors on silk. H. 104.2 cm., W. 74.8 cm.
Fenollosa-Weld Collection. 11.4400

Kano Tanyū was one of the most gifted masters among the large Kano family of painters. One of the finest works attributable to his hand is this central icon of a triptych representing Confucius at the so-called Apricot Altar, flanked by his pupils Yen Hui and Tseng-tzŭ. It is executed in the strong, thick and brilliant brushwork which is associated with this master and gives the great sage the dignity and authority which Confucian scholars, in China as well as in Japan, attributed to him. The solemn character of the paintings suggests that they were ritual icons, used in the semiannual *sekiten* ceremony held in Confucian academies.

According to Fenollosa, who acquired the set in 1882 from the last artist of Tanyū's line of succession, Kano Tambi, the paintings are copies by Tanyū after an earlier set by Kano Masanobu, at one time kept in the Sage's Hall or Seidō of the Ashikaga College. As the Masanobu set seems to have disappeared, we have no way to document this highly interesting pedigree. However, Tanyū's painting shows an unmistakable resemblance to a Japanese wooden statue of Confucius (which Fenollosa mistook for Chinese) which is inscribed and dated in accordance with A.D. 1534. This fine statue, of which only the fan is lacking now, is still preserved in the Ashikaga College.

Published: Ernest F. Fenollosa, *Epochs of Chinese and Japanese Art*, New York and London, 1913, p. 93.

57–58
UTATANE NO E-ZŌSHI
Japan, Ashikaga period, 16th century
Ink on paper. Two handscrolls, H. 13.5 cm., L. 519 and 517.6 cm.
William Sturgis Bigelow Collection. 11.9456–9457

The artist has reproduced the text of the romantic love story *Utatane zōshi*, which dates from about the middle of the Ashikaga period, on long, narrow strips of paper, mounted in two handscrolls. Interspersed between the long passages of text are the illustrations, minutely drawn in black Japanese ink. These delicate and often poetically sensitive paintings are late examples of a genre known as *monogatari-e*, i.e. illustrations of love stories, often written by women, modeled upon the great classics of the Heian period such as the *Tale of Genji* and the *Makura no Sōshi*. The title of the *Utatane zōshi* is actually based on a poem of Ono no Komachi, one of the Six Poets.

Like the contents, its illustrations recall the style of the Heian period and show numerous stylistic and compositional archaisms. It would seem that the artist was inspired by such prototypes as the Toyonoakari E-zōshi (thirteenth to fourteenth century). According to the documents which accompany this pair of scrolls, both the calligraphy and the illustrations are supposed to be the work of a certain Asukai Masako, a daughter of the well-known poet and calligrapher Asukai Masachika (1417–1490). Another set of scrolls, illustrating the same story, is now in the Freer Gallery of Art, Washington, D.C.

59–60
Soga Shōhaku (1730–1781)
THE FOUR GREYBEARDS OF MOUNT SHANG
Japan, Edo period, 18th century
Ink on paper with gold dust. Pair of six-fold screens,
H. 156.2 cm., W. 60.6 cm. (each panel)
Fenollosa-Weld Collection. 11.4513–4514

In this masterwork of his later years the "fanatic" painter Soga Shōhaku injects new life into a theme which generations of *suiboku* and Kano artists had made into a dreary convention. The Four Greybeards; T'ang Hsüan-ming, Ch'i Li-chi, Ts'ui Kuang, and Chou Shu; who had retired to Mount Shang during the reign of the tyrant Ch'in Shih-huang-ti (221–210 B.C.) were famous paragons of loyalty, and Japanese artists had traditionally treated the theme of their retirement from public life with respect. Shōhaku, however, makes them look like down-and-out characters who kill time drinking wine under a huge gnarled pine tree. Nevertheless, this bizarre and grotesque rendering, executed in a few sweeping, but superbly controlled brushstrokes, certainly was not meant to ridicule these ancient heroes. Shōhaku was, after all, a staunch traditionalist who looked to the past for inspiration. He must have painted these quaint figures in order to evoke a spirit of great antiquity, dating back to a period long before the dawn of Japanese civilization. The liberal sprinkling of gold dust, applied at a later time, does not distract the eye from this extraordinarily powerful display of dynamic brushwork.

61
MONGOLIAN YOUTH
China, late Chou period, ca. 4th-3rd century B.C.
Bronze figure and jade birds. H. 28.5 cm.
Maria Antoinette Evans Fund. 31.976

This superb example of early Chinese bronze sculpture shows a young man intently gazing at two birds chained to the top of two sticks which he holds vertically in his hands. The figure reveals many details of the dress and hairstyle of the period and is therefore not only a fascinating work of art, but also an important source of evidence for early Chinese cultural history. The figure is said to have been excavated at Chin-ts'un near Lo-yang (Honan province). Although there is no definite proof of this claim, the figure does seem to fit well into the elegant style of the objects which are usually associated with this site.

Published: Sueji Umehara, *Rakuyō Kinson Kobo Shūei*, Kyoto, 1937, Pl. XXXI.

62
KUAN-YIN
China, late Northern Chou or early Sui period, ca. A.D. 580
Gray limestone with traces of polychromy. H. 249 cm.
Francis Bartlett Fund. 15.254

This exceptionally large and fine sculpture of Kuan-yin (Sanskrit: Avalokiteśvara) represents a type of sculpture which is typical of the style of the second half of the sixth century. Standing on a lotus, which has been placed on a square base with lions at the corners, the figure holds a cluster of lotus buds in the left hand. The gently flowing draperies are richly adorned with different kinds of jewelry.

The sculpture was discovered in October, 1909, by Okakura Kakuzō's nephew, Hayasaki Kōkichi, who found it standing partially buried in the grounds of the Old Stone Buddha Temple (Ku Shih-fo-ssŭ) near Sian, the capital of Shensi province. Many Japanese scholars have maintained that this temple stands on the site of the famous T'ang temple, Ch'ing-lung-ssŭ (Blue Dragon Monastery). This temple was founded in A.D. 582 and in subsequent centuries often served as a place of residence for such famous Japanese pilgrims as Kōbō Daishi. However, there is a discrepancy between the exact location of this temple and the site of the Ku Shih-fo-ssŭ, and a recent survey by Chinese archaeologists (*Kaogu*, 1964, no. 7) suggests that the actual site of the Ch'ing-lung-ssŭ should be sought some distance to the west.

A smaller standing Avalokiteśvara in the Minneapolis Institute of Arts, dated in accordance with A.D. 570 and inscribed again after restoration in A.D. 582 is closely related to our sculpture, which in all likelihood dates from the early years of the Sui period.

Published: Osvald Sirén, *Chinese Sculpture*, London, 1925, Pl. 274.

63
BODHISATTVA
China, early Eastern Wei period, ca. A.D. 530
Gray limestone, yellowed by burial. H. 196.5 cm.
Gift of Denman Waldo Ross in memory of Okakura Kakuzō. 13.2804

One of the largest early pieces of stone sculpture ever to come out of China, this finely carved figure shows a close resemblance to the sculptures of the cave temple complex of Lung-mên, especially to those of cave XXIV, which can be dated by inscription to A.D. 527. The cuspidate necklace is identical with those of the figures in this cave, but the softly flowing folds of the drapery suggest a slightly later date, possibly in the early years of the Eastern Wei period. The details of the back are partially carved, an indication that the figure was not originally part of a cave temple.

In the spring of 1903 the Japanese painter and amateur archaeologist, Hayasaki Kōkichi, visited the temple Pai-ma-ssŭ near Lo-yang and saw a group of Chinese excavate this sculpture from the central courtyard of the temple. Although he and Okakura Kakuzō repeatedly tried to acquire it, the sculpture disappeared from the temple, to reappear in Paris shortly before Okakura's death.

Published: Seigai Ōmura, *Shina Bijutsushi Chōsohen*, Tokyo, 1915, Pl. 552; Osvald Sirén, *Chinese Sculpture*, London, 1925, Pl. 112.

64
KUAN-YIN
China, Sung period, ca. 12th century
Polychromed wood. H. 141 cm.
Harvey Edward Wetzel Fund. 20.590

The compassionate Bodhisattva Kuan-yin (Sanskrit: Avalokiteśvara) is represented in the Posture of Royal Relaxation (Sanskrit: *Mahārājalīla*), the right arm supported by the raised right knee, the left leg hanging down and the head slightly inclined. During the reign of the Sung dynasty and that of its successor in the North, the Chin, this type of wooden sculpture became common in the Northern parts of China, especially in the province of Shansi.

During restoration a thick layer of later overpainting was removed from the image, revealing bright colors as well as *kirigane* (cut gold foil) designs underneath. As a result, the original resplendent quality of the image is now again apparent. Images of this type were commonly placed in front of brightly colored wall-paintings representing the legendary abode of Avalokiteśvara at Potalaka.

65
YAKSA YŎRAE
Korea, Unified Silla Dynasty, ca. 8th century
Gilt bronze. H. 36 cm.
Gift of Edward J. Holmes in memory of his mother Mrs. W. Scott Fitz. 32.436

This elegant statue of Yaksa Yŏrae (Sanskrit: Bhaiṣajya-guru) shows the Korean adaptation of the T'ang style in its most classic form. The fine details of the elaborate lotus stand and the balanced proportions of the standing figure are typical of the Silla style of the eighth century. It antedates the period during which a more ponderous style of figures with disproportionately large heads prevailed.

For many years this statue was in the private collection of Okakura Kakuzō.

Published: Chōsen Koseki Zufu, Vol. V, Tokyo, 1917, Pl. 617.

66
ANIMAL FIGHT IN THE SHANG-LIN PARK
China, Han period, ca. 1st century A.D.
Hollow tiles, painted in colors. W. 240.7 cm., H. 73.8 cm., DEPTH 13.5 cm. (measurements of complete piece)
Denman Waldo Ross Collection. 25.10–13, 25.190

This set of tiles, consisting of five pieces, forms a tympanum. It was excavated during the First World War from a four-chambered tomb located about eight *li* west of the present city of Lo-yang (Honan province). The figure scenes painted on it represent men watching fighting animals, presumably the *tou-shou* (animal fights) staged at the Royal Zoological Park of the Han, the Shang-lin Park. Although parts of the surface had deteriorated before the tiles came to Boston, the excellent draftsmanship of the supple and lively brushwork, together with the delicate coloring are still clearly visible.

In 1957, Chinese archaeologists excavated a tomb not far from the original location of the Boston tiles. The tympanum in the main burial chamber differs from our piece in that the two triangular sections and the central square slab have a reticulated decoration, but the painted figures on the lower crossbeam are closely related to those on our piece. The fact that our piece is decorated on both sides suggests that it was used, like the recently discovered piece, as the tympanum of of a partition between the two parts of the main burial chamber which could be viewed from both sides. As a result of their study comparing architectural features, the excavators of the recently found tomb date it in the last half of the first century B.C. This is considerably earlier than the dates previously suggested for our piece, which range from the second to the fourth century of our era.

Published: Kojiro Tomita, *Portfolio of Chinese Paintings in the Museum (Han to Sung periods)*, Boston, 1933, Pls. 1–8.

67–69
Attributed to Yen Li-pên (died 673)
THE THIRTEEN EMPERORS
China, T'ang period, 7th century
Handscroll, ink and colors on silk. H. 51.3 cm., L. 531 cm.
Denman Waldo Ross Collection. 31.643

The scroll consists of a series of portraits of thirteen emperors and their attendants. The criteria used in making the selection are unclear, for the personnages do not seem to have been chosen for their historical importance. The earliest is an emperor of the Former Han dynasty, the latest is the second Emperor of the Sui dynasty. The first six portraits (the emperors are not represented in their exact chronological order) are obviously copies, made to reproduce a missing section of the scroll. This section probably dates from the Northern Sung period. The other seven portraits, however, are of a much earlier period and may well date from the seventh century. This was the period when the celebrated court painter, Yen Li-pên, was active, and the scroll was attributed to this master at least as early as Northern Sung times. There is nothing in the style of painting which would contradict this early attribution. On the contrary, the lack of a background, the sensitive brushwork, the soft coloring, and the decorative shading all indicate an early date and make this handscroll one of the great masterpieces of early Chinese figure painting.

Published: Kojiro Tomita, *Portfolio of Chinese Paintings in the Museum (Han to Sung periods)*, Boston, 1933, Pls. 10–24.

70
Emperor Sung Hui-tsung (1082–1135)
THE FIVE-COLORED PARAKEET
China, Sung period, early 12th century
Handscroll, ink and colors on silk. H. 53.3 cm., L. 125.1 cm.
Maria Antoinette Evans Fund. 33.364

Among the treasures of the Department of Asiatic Art are two paintings by the Emperor-painter, Hui-tsung, of the Sung dynasty, a gifted artist whose tragic life ended while he was in the captivity of the Jurčen tribe in Manchuria. This painting dates from the time he was still his own master. It represents a five-colored parakeet which the Emperor kept in his palace garden. In order to commemorate this event, he painted a sensitive and accurate likeness of this exotic bird and composed a poem, which is added to the painting in his elegant hand.

The painting carries the seal and a partly obliterated signature of the artist. It was once in the collection of the Mongol Emperor, Wên-tsung (reigned 1329–1332). Although there is considerable uncertainty as to which of several extant paintings of birds were actually painted by Hui-tsung, this painting is undoubtedly one of the finest of this type and is most likely a work executed by the imperial artist himself.

Published: Kojiro Tomita, "The Five-colored Parakeet By Hui-tsung (1082–1135)," *MFA Bulletin*, XXXI, 187 (1933), 75–79.

71–72
Emperor Sung Hui-tsung (1082–1135)
LADIES PREPARING NEWLY WOVEN SILK
China, Sung period, early 12th century
Handscroll, ink and colors on silk. H. 37 cm., L. 145.3 cm.
Chinese and Japanese Special Fund. 12.886

The second work by Hui-tsung in the collection of the Museum of Fine Arts is the result of a combination of two of the Emperor's interests, painting and collecting. Although unsigned, the painting carries an inscription by Chang-tsung, Emperor of the Chin dynasty (reigned 1188–1208) who attributes the painting to Hui-tsung and who calls it a copy after a painting by the T'ang artist Chang Hsüan (first half of the eighth century) which was in Hui-tsung's vast collection. The fact that Hui-tsung was the maternal grand-father of Chang-tsung, and that Chang-tsung may therefore have been in a good position to judge the authenticity and provenance of this painting, adds considerable weight to this early attribution.

The original by Chang Hsüan, recorded in the *Hsüan-ho hua-p'u*, the catalogue of Hui-tsung's collection, has been lost, and we have no way of judging how scrupulously Hui-tsung copied the original. That at least the method of ironing the new silk did not change in the course of the centuries which separate Chang Hsüan from Hui-tsung is evident from a wall-painting in a tomb at Shih-chia-chuang in Hopei province (see *Kaogu Xuebao*, 1962, no. 2, color plate). Like Yen Li-pên's Emperors (see Pls. 67–69), the ladies, dressed in the same fashion as some of the T'ang tomb figurines, stand in empty space. In a dignified manner they go about their tasks of pounding the silk and drawing out the thread. The unusually bright colors of the scroll may represent the preservation of one of the stylistic features of T'ang period figure painting.

Published: Kojiro Tomita, *Portfolio of Chinese Paintings in the Museum (Han to Sung periods)*, Boston, 1933, 46 and 52–55.

73
Ch'ên Yung-chih (flourished ca. 1023)
BUDDHA UNDER THE MANGO TREE
China, Sung period, ca. 1025
Ink and colors and gold on paper. H. 211 cm., W. 71.2 cm.
Keith McLeod Fund. 56.256

This painting represents a miracle which Gautama Buddha performed as a preliminary to the Great Miracle of Śrāvastī. At the command of the Buddha the gardener Ganda planted a mango seed, whereupon a mango tree sprang up immediately. Almost instantly it was covered with flowers and fruit (see Eugene W. Burlingame, *Buddhist Legends*, Part 3, Cambridge, Mass., 1921, p. 41). The Buddha, who holds a mango in his hand, is dressed in a red robe which is drawn in closely spaced undulating lines of ink and gold. The luxuriant tree winds upward in powerful curves. The pigments in which the rocks, trees, leaves, and fruit are rendered have been piled up so as to create a low relief. The style of the drapery and this unusual relief technique have both been traditionally associated with the Central Asian painter, Yü-ch'ih I-seng (first half of the seventh century). The painting was attributed to this celebrated master until recently when a signature was discovered in the lower left corner reading: "respectfully copied by Ch'ên Yung-chih." It is probable that Ch'ên Yung-chih, an early eleventh century court artist, copied the painting from a work of Yü-chih I-sêng, possibly one from the imperial collection.

Numerous seals allow us to trace back its pedigree to the collection of Yang Shih (1053–1135) and to that of Sung Hui-tsung. Recently a thick coat of a brown glue-like substance was removed, revealing for the first time the brilliance of the original colors.

Published: Hsien-ch'i Tseng, *Loan Exhibition of Chinese Paintings*, Toronto, Royal Ontario Museum, 1956, no. 1.

74

Traditionally attributed to Yen Li-pên
SCHOLARS OF THE NORTHERN CH'I COLLATING THE CLASSICS
China, Sung period, ca. 11th century
Handscroll, ink and colors on silk. H. 27.6 cm., L. 114 cm.
Denman Waldo Ross Collection. 31.123

In the seventh year of the T'ien-pao era, A.D. 556, the Emperor Wên-hsüan-ti of the Northern Ch'i dynasty ordered the scholar Fan Sun and eleven associates to collate the texts of the Chinese Classics for the use of the heir-apparent. This event, a milestone in the history of Chinese bibliography, became a favorite subject for pictorial representation. The present painting consists only of part of the original work and shows only five of the twelve scholars.

The extraordinary quality of the drawing, especially of the faces, and the delicate coloring clearly point to a master of considerable talent. Fan Ch'êng-ta (1126–1193), the well-known Sung scholar who was the first to add a colophon to the scroll, associated the theme with Yen Li-pên, to whom the painting was henceforth attributed. It is more likely, however, that the painting is a work by a Northern Sung figure-painter, based, perhaps, on a T'ang period prototype.

Published: Kojiro Tomita, "Scholars of the Northern Ch'i Dynasty Collating Classic Texts," *MFA Bulletin*, XXIX, 174 (1931), 58–63.

75

WÊN-CHI'S RETURN TO CHINA
China, Sung/Chin periods, 12th century
Four album leaves, ink and colors on silk. H. 24.8 cm., w. 46.3 cm. (measurements of 28.63)
Denman Waldo Ross Collection. 28.62–65

The story of Lady Wên-chi's captivity in Mongolia and her return to China twelve years later, after she had been forced to abandon her Hsiung-nu husband and her children, is one of the typical northern frontier stories of the Han period. Poets and painters have often used this dramatic episode in their works, especially, it would seem, during periods of foreign supremacy.

The four album leaves in the collection were originally part of a series of eighteen, a number obviously derived from the number of Lady Wên-chi's poems. The Encampment by a Stream (28.63) shows Wên-chi and her "barbarian" husband sitting under a roof-shaped tent which has been set up in front of their dome-shaped yurt. On the left servants are preparing food. The anonymous artist has placed this Han drama in a contemporary setting. The enemies of his own lifetime, the Jurčen, have served as examples for the Huns of the distant past. His attention to the illustrative detail has made this set of leaves an interesting document for the study of frontier life during the Sung period.

Published: Kojiro Tomita, "Wên-chi's Captivity in Mongolia and Her Return to China," *MFA Bulletin*, XXVI, 155 (1928), 40–45.

76

Chao Po-chü (first half of the 12th century)
ENTRY OF HAN KAO-TSU INTO KUAN-CHUNG
China, Sung period, 12th century
Handscroll, ink and colors on silk. H. 29.7 cm., L. 312.8 cm.
William Amory Gardner and Annie A. Hough Funds. 31.910

Chao Po-chü, a relative of the imperial Sung house, was one of the painters who followed the Imperial family to the south after the fall of the Northern Capital K'ai-fêng in 1126. He soon became one of the favorite court artists, specializing in blue-and-green landscapes and architectural paintings in an archaic style. In this handscroll he has depicted a historical theme based on an incident in the eventful career of the insurgent Liu Pang (247–195 B.C.) who was to become the first emperor of the Han dynasty. The last section of the scroll illustrated here shows him surrounded by his council of war in a palace at Kuan-chung, a Ch'in stronghold which he conquered and held for a brief span of time in 202 B.C. The signature at the end of the scroll indicates that the painting was presented to an emperor, presumably Sung Kao-tsung (reigned 1127–1162).

Published: Kojiro Tomita, "Entry of the First Emperor of the Han Dynasty into Kuan-chung," *MFA Bulletin*, XXX, 181 (1932), 69–72.

77

Chou Chi-ch'ang (second half of the 12th century)
ARHATS BESTOWING ALMS UPON BEGGARS
China, Sung period, 1184
Ink and colors on silk. H. 111.5 cm., W. 53.1 cm.
General Fund. 95.4

This painting, together with nine others in the collection, was originally part of a set of one hundred paintings showing the Five Hundred Arhats. The set belongs to the Daitokuji in Kyoto. Forty-four of these were exhibited in the United States in a traveling exhibition organized by Ernest Fenollosa in 1894. At the close of the exhibition the Museum of Fine Arts acquired ten of these paintings, while two additional paintings, not included in that exhibition, were sold to Charles L. Freer and are now in the Freer Gallery of Art, Washington, D.C. At present the temple still has eighty-two paintings.

Some of the paintings bear dedicatory inscriptions in gold which indicate that the set was made between 1178 and 1184 for the temple Hui-an-yüan, near Ning-po (Chêkiang province). Some of them are signed by Chou Chi-ch'ang, others by Lin T'ing-kuei, both of whom were probably professional painters. The set was taken to Japan during the thirteenth century and came to play an important role in the iconographical evolution of Japanese paintings representing Arhats. The entire set was copied by the famous monk-painter, Minchō (1352–1431), in 1386; this set is now preserved in the Tōfukuji, Kyoto.

Published: Wen Fong, *The Lohans and a Bridge to Heaven*, Washington, 1958.

78

Ch'ên Jung (flourished 1210–1260)
THE NINE DRAGONS
China, Sung period, 1244
Handscroll, ink with touches of red on paper. H. 46.3 cm., L. 1096.4 cm.
Francis Gardner Curtis Fund. 17.1697

In an extraordinary display of powerful and versatile brush-work, the artist has painted nine dragons of different types and in varying poses, sporting among clouds and waves. The artist, who was famous for this genre, added two inscriptions, from one of which we learn that he painted this scroll in the year 1244. This painting stands out among several

similar works attributed to Ch'ên Jung as a superb example of the artist's great talent. The Museum also owns part of another dragon scroll which is attributed to Ch'ên Jung.

Published: Hsien-ch'i Tseng, "A Study of the Nine Dragons Scroll," *Archives of the Chinese Art Society of America*, vol. XI (1957), 17–35.

79

Traditionally attributed to Tung Yüan (907–960)
CLEAR WEATHER IN THE VALLEY
China, Sung period, 12th–15th century
Handscroll, ink and slight colors on paper. H. 37.5 cm., W. 150.8 cm.
Chinese and Japanese Special Fund. 12.903

This masterpiece of early Chinese landscape painting, acquired for the Museum in China by Hayasaki Kōkichi, has for many centuries been attributed to the tenth century master Tung Yüan. Although we have no firsthand knowledge of the stylistic characteristics of Tung Yüan's work, the present handscroll would seem to breathe a spirit which is different from the few surviving tenth century landscapes. The traditional attribution is therefore not likely to be correct. It is a typical example of the so-called "level distance" composition, which was first perfected by Tung Yüan and Li Ch'êng. Painted with a superb feeling for atmospheric perspective, it reveals a poetic sentiment which is often found in landscapes of the Southern Sung period.

Published: Kojiro Tomita, *Portfolio of Chinese Paintings in the Museum (Han to Sung periods)*, Boston, 1933, Pls. 33–36.

80

Ma Yüan (active 1190–1225)
BARE WILLOWS AND DISTANT MOUNTAINS
China, Sung period, ca. 1200
Fan-shaped album leaf, mounted as hanging scroll, ink and colors on silk. H. 23.8 cm., W. 24.2 cm.
Chinese and Japanese Special Fund. 14.61

The Northern Sung artists sought to convey the grandeur of the forces of nature in their landscapes; the artists of the Southern Sung, of whom Ma Yüan was one of the most distinguished, had a different approach to their environment. They stressed its peaceful aspects and its poetic qualities. The Bare Willows and Distant Mountains is a typical example of this new attitude and one of the finest works of this famous master, whose trimmed signature appears in the lower right corner.

Published: Kojiro Tomita, *Portfolio of Chinese Paintings in the Museum (Han to Sung Periods)*, Boston, 1933, Pl. 94.

81

Wang Yüan-ch'i (1642–1715)

SPRING MORNING AT YEN-T'AN

China, Ch'ing period, 1711

Handscroll, ink and slight colors on paper. H. 38 cm.,

L. 304.7 cm.

Keith McLeod Fund. 56.10

Wang Yüan-ch'i, who was a noted court official during the Ch'ing dynasty, has here represented the scenery along the Ch'ien-t'ang river in Chêkiang, utilizing a combination of dry brushstrokes over a light, wet under-drawing. He was the last of the "Four Wangs" and was one of the leading theoreticians of the conservative Lou-tung school. His work, always a free adaptation of some distant Yüan prototype, is as conventional as his ideas were, but the fact that he was here painting for a friend gives a personal and sensitive touch to his often somewhat arid style.

Published: Kojiro Tomita and Hsien-ch'i Tseng, *Portfolio of Chinese Paintings in the Museum (Yüan to Ch'ing Periods)*, Boston, 1961, Pls. 147–148.

82

JAR WITH COVER

China, Late Chou dynasty, 5th–3rd century B.C.

Pottery decorated with glass paste. H. 11.6 cm., D. 13.9 cm.

Charles B. Hoyt Collection. 50.1841

A repeated design of round medallions in square frames has been applied in glass paste on the buff pottery ground. The bright colors of the glass have faded into soft green and gray. Two other pieces of this rare type of late Chou pottery are known to exist. One is now in the British Museum, London; the other piece is in the William Rockhill Nelson Gallery of Art, Kansas City, Missouri.

Published: Sueji Umehara, "Antique Chinese Potteries decorated with Glass Paste," *Yamato Bunka*, No. 15, September, 1954, pp. 8–13.

83

EWER

China, Northern Sung period, ca. 11th century

So-called Tung ware. H. 19.7 cm., D. 16.2 cm.

Charles B. Hoyt Collection. 50.2009

An elegant design of peony leaves has been carved in relief in the gray body of this globular ewer. Pieces of a similar type with the same handle shape and double spout have been identified by some scholars as belonging to a rare ceramic type of the Northern Sung period, which is characterized by a dull, grayish-green glaze and which is referred

to in the *Ko-ku yao-lun* as "Tung-yao," possibly some Northern Sung official *(kuan)* ware.

84

JAR (WAN-NIEN-HU)

China, T'ang period, 7th–8th century

Green, blue, and white glazed ware. H. 28.2 cm., D. 25.9 cm.

Charles B. Hoyt Collection. 50.879

Jars of this type, popularly known as *wan-nien-hu*, were used for the storage of grain and are fairly common among the mortuary gifts placed in T'ang tombs. The green, blue, and white glazes have been arranged in chevron patterns, reaching halfway down the lower half of the ovoid body of the jar.

Published: Sekai Tōji Zenshū, Vol. 9, Tokyo, 1956, 197, fig. 88.

85

CEREMONIAL BOWL AND STAND

China, Northern Sung period, ca. 11th century

Northern celadon or Yao-chou yao. H. 21.6 cm., D. of bowl 17 cm.

Charles B. Hoyt Collection. 50.939 and 50.943

The bowl stands on a base with five mask-headed feet and a wide, curving rim. The inside of the bowl is decorated with nine dragon heads which are modeled around a reticulated dome. Finely carved flower scrolls cover the curved rim of the stand and the outside of the bowl. The gray clay body, burnt red where exposed to the fire, is covered with an olive-green glaze. The mask-headed feet are very similar to those on a piece which was excavated recently from a kiln site at Huang-pao-chên (see *Kaogu*, 1959, no. 12) in Shensi province. The kiln site is located in the district which was called Yao-chou in Sung times; hence the ware is now often referred to as Yao-chou yao.

Published: Jan Fontein and Rose Hempel, *China, Korea, Japan*, Berlin, 1968, Pl. 53.

86

WINE BOTTLE

China, Northern Sung period, 11th–12th century

Tz'ŭ-chou type ware. H. 39.1 cm., D. 19.6 cm.

Charles B. Hoyt Collection. 50.1058

The pearl-punched ground for the incised decoration, which has been filled in with a reddish-brown color, is typical of the products of the kilns of Ch'ü-ho in Têng-fêng-hsien and near Mi-hsien (Honan province), an important center for the production of Tz'ŭ-chou type wares during the Sung period. Around the short neck is a floral design, and on the central band of the vase are three figures carrying gourds on sticks over their shoulders.

87

VASE

China, Northern Sung period, 11th–12th century
Tz'ŭ-chou type ware. H. 42.8 cm., D. 20.3 cm.
Charles B. Hoyt Collection. 50.1056

This ovoid vase with a long neck and wide, saucer-shaped mouth is covered with a carved decoration of peonies and lotus leaves, which is partially cut through the white slip to the stained clay body. This technique is typical for wares of the Tz'ŭ-chou type which were made all over Northern China during the Sung period. The exact provenance of this type has not yet been firmly established. Koyama Fujio has described this vase as a product of the Hsiu-wu kilns at Tang-yang-yü (Honan province), but recently Ch'ên Wan-li has published a similar piece as a product of the kilns in Têng-fêng hsien (cf. *Sung-tai Pei-fang min-chien tz'ŭ-ch'i*, Pl. 19).

Published: Rakuji Hasebe, *Sō no Jishū-yō, Tōki Zenshū,* Vol. 13, Tokyo, 1958, Pl. 30.

88

COVERED VASE

China, Yüan period, second half of the 14th century
Porcelain decorated in underglaze blue. H. (with cover) 38 cm.
Clara Bertram Kimball Collection. 37.292

The peony scrolls on the shoulder of this vase and the lotus panels along the base, are both common decorative motifs on fourteenth century blue and white porcelain. The central zone shows figures in a landscape. Recent research by Saitō Kikutarō has revealed that the decoration of this and a few other vases of a similar type is based on scenes of Yüan theater plays. On this vase the great heroes of the Period of the Three Kingdoms (third century A.D.) are shown. The side illustrated here shows Chu-ko Liang in his straw hut; on the other side Kuan Yü, Chang Fei and Liu Pei are shown after they had sworn their oath of brotherly allegiance in the Peach Orchard.

Although now generally called mei-p'ing, i.e., prunus vase, the truncated cone cover with a lotus knob suggests that the vase may actually have been used as a container for liquids.

Published: Sir Harry Garner, *Oriental Blue and White,* London, 1954, Pl. 19; Saitō Kikutarō, "Gendai Sometsuke Kō II" ("A Study of Yüan Blue and White, II"), *Kobijutsu,* no. 19 (October 1967), pp. 65 ff.

89

VASE (MAEBYŎNG)

Korea, Koryŏ period, 11th–12th century
Celadon, carved decoration. H. 35.3 cm., D. 23.2 cm.
Special Korean Pottery Fund. 11.1821

The body of the vase is covered with a carved decoration of dragons rising up from among the clouds and waves. The even glaze and the fine carving make this vase one of the finest pieces of its type. It was bought for the Museum by Langdon Warner during one of this trips to Japan.

90

VASE (MAEBYŎNG)

Korea, Koryŏ period, 12th century
Celadon, inlaid decoration. H. 31.1 cm., D. 18.1 cm.
Charles B. Hoyt Collection. 50.989

The vase is decorated with a simple design of cranes and bamboo executed in inlaid white and black slip. The simplicity of the design indicates that this vase is one of the relatively early examples of inlaid celadon, made not long after this technique was first developed and perfected.

91

CROWN

China, Liao period, 10th–11th century
Silver gilt, repoussé decoration. H. 20.6 cm., CIR. 62 cm.
William Sturgis Bigelow Collection, by exchange. 40.749

The traditional motif of two dragons chasing a flaming pearl has been executed in repoussé against a background of stylized waves and clouds. The piece, which came to the Museum as a plaque, was reshaped into a crown after the publication of a piece of the same type, excavated at the village of Chang-chia Ying-tzŭ (Chien-p'ing district, Liao-ning province) in 1956.

The provenance of this piece is somewhat uncertain. On the one hand, the rendering of the highly traditional Chinese motif has a slightly unusual flavor, and originally the crown was therefore attributed to Korea. However, the same motif, rendered in exactly the same style, appears on a silver saddle decoration, excavated in 1953 from another Manchurian tomb of the Liao period (see *Kaogu Xuebao,* 1956, no. 3, pp. 1–32). It is known from Chinese official records that such silver gilt saddle decorations were among the ceremonial gifts which the Chinese presented to Jurčen royalty on several occasions.

From the location in the tomb where the crown from Chang-chia Ying-tzŭ was found, it would seem that the crowns were used as ceremonial headgear for the dead. Two rectangular perforations at both ends of the plaque suggest that a ribbon or shawl was used to adjust the crown to the wearer's head.

Published: Robert T. Paine, "A Crown of the Liao Dynasty," *MFA Bulletin,* LXII, 328 (1964), 44–47.

92
EWER AND BASIN
Korea, Koryŏ period, 11th–12th century
Silver, parcel gilt. H. of ewer 33.7 cm., H. of basin 17 cm.,
D. of basin 18.9 cm.
Helen and Alice Colburn Fund. 35.646

The scalloped body, the spout, and the handle of the ewer all have shapes inspired by bamboo forms. The cover consists of three conventionalized lotuses, surmounted by a phoenix. The ewer fits into a basin of similarly scalloped shape; both vessels are engraved with a decoration of floral sprays. Their shapes are very similar to those of ceramic types from Korea as well as from Northern Sung China.

Published: Kojiro Tomita, "A Koryŏ Silver Ewer of about the Eleventh Century," *MFA Bulletin,* XXXIII, 199 (1935), 66–69.

93
ALTARPIECE WITH AMITĀBHA AND ATTENDANTS
China, Sui period, A.D. 593
Bronze, partially covered with green patination. H. 76.5 cm.
Gift of Mrs. W. Scott Fitz (22.407) and gift of Edward Jackson Holmes in memory of his mother Mrs. W. Scott Fitz (47.1407–1412)

This elaborate representation of the Western Paradise is a masterpiece of bronze casting of the Sui period. The only other piece of this type which has been preserved is a much less complete altarpiece in the Shanghai Museum (see Werner and Bedřich Forman, *Ancient Relics of China,* Peking, 1962, Pl. 101). The principal figure is the Buddha Amitābha, seated on a reticulated lotus throne. Above it is a flowering tree over which the Seven Buddhas of the Past hover, and around which apsaras fly. On each side stand three figures: a figure with a coiled headdress (probably representing a Pratyeka Buddha), a disciple of the Buddha, and a Bodhisattva. The disciples are probably Ānanda and Mahākāśyapa, the Bodhisattvas are Kuan-yin (Sanskrit: Avalokiteśvara) and Ta-shih-chih (Sanskrit: Mahāsthāmaprāpta). These figures are all detachable, as are the two Guardian Kings, the two lions, and the incense burner in front.

This altar was excavated, probably during the first years of this century, at a place about five miles to the southeast of the town of Chao-hsien in the province of Hopei. The Guardian Kings, the lions, and the incense burner on the

front were removed after its discovery shortly before the altar came into the posession of the Viceroy Tuan Fang. They were reunited with the altar only after it had been in Boston twenty-five years.

Published: Kojiro Tomita, "The Chinese Bronze Buddhist Group of A.D. 593 and its Original Arrangement," *MFA Bulletin,* XLII, 252 (1945), 14–19.

94
LION
China, T'ang period, late 7th century
Limestone. H. 112 cm.
Rebecca Richardson Joslin Fund. 40.70

This sculpture was removed from the wall of the vestibule of Cave IX of the cave temple complex at Lung-mên. The other lion from this site is now in the William Rockhill Nelson Gallery of Art, Kansas City, Missouri. An inscription in this cave dates from A.D. 680 and this is thought to be the approximate date of most of the sculpture in it.

Published: Kojiro Tomita, "Two Chinese Sculptures from Lung-mên," *MFA Bulletin,* XXXV, 207 (1937), 2–4.

95
COVERED JAR
China, Sung period, 10th–11th century
Yüeh ware. H. 38 cm., D. 17.7 cm.
Charles B. Hoyt Collection. 50.1048

The vase has an ovoid body; a tall, contracted neck with two loops on the shoulder; and an everted mouth. It is covered with a lid with a reticulated knob. The body has an all-over incised decoration of lotus petals; the entire piece is covered with a grayish, crackled, green glaze. This jar is a more elegant and perhaps somewhat earlier version of a ceramic type which can be dated by an inscribed example in the David Foundation in London, dated Yüan-feng 2nd year (A.D. 1080).

96
Chao Ling-jang (ca. 1080–1100)
SUMMER MIST ALONG THE LAKE SHORE
China, Sung period, A.D. 1100
Handscroll, ink and colors on silk. H. 19.1 cm., L. 161.3 cm.
Keith McLeod Fund. 57.724

Chao Ling-jang, a member of the Imperial Sung family, is a typical representative of the landscape painters of the Academy of K'ai-fêng. In his misty landscapes geese are the only living beings. No steep mountains rise up, for the painter's intention was to evoke the atmosphere of the plains in the vicinity of the capital. An air of pleasant repose

184

and simple charm pervades his work. Very few paintings by Chao Ling-jang have survived. This scroll, signed and dated in accordance with A.D. 1100, and once part of the Imperial Manchu Household Collection, is one of the rare paintings generally accepted as a work of this master.

Published: Kokka, no. 494.

97
Wang Chên-p'êng (first half of the 14th century)
Mahāprajāpatī Holding the Infant Buddha
China, Yüan period, 14th century
Handscroll, ink on silk. H. 31.9 cm., L. 94.4 cm.
Chinese and Japanese Special Fund. 12.902

Mahāprajāpatī, the younger sister of Queen Māyā, became Siddhārtha's foster mother when his mother died seven days after giving birth to him. The painting shows her holding the infant. She is surrounded by five attendants, one of whom feeds a lion, a possible reference to the lion's roar which symbolizes the Buddha's preaching of the Buddhist Law.

Here, the artist, who is known best for his detailed architectural paintings (Chinese: *chieh-hua*), has applied his meticulous technique to a figure scene. His signature is hidden among the ink spots which form the bark of a tree on the right.

Published: Kojiro Tomita, "Two Chinese Paintings Depicting the Infant Buddha and Mahāprajāpatī," *MFA Bulletin*, XLII, 247 (1944), 15–20.

98–99
Attributed to Sung Kao-tsung (1107–1187) and Ma Ho-chih (12th century)
Six Odes of the Mao-shih
China, Sung period, 12th century
Handscroll, ink and colors on silk. H. 27 cm., L. 383.8 cm.
Marshall H. Gould Fund. 51.698

Six odes from the Hsiao-ya section of the Book of Odes, the *Shih-ching*, are inscribed on the scroll. The calligraphy is attributed to the Sung Emperor Kao-tsung. Each ode is accompanied by an illustration which is attributed to Ma Ho-chih. This artist is known chiefly as the court artist who was ordered to illustrate copies of the *Shih-ching* written by Kao-tsung. Many copies exist, and it is often difficult to decide which of these were actually written by Kao-tsung and illustrated by Ma Ho-chih, for other calligraphers and painters appear to have continued the project which these two never finished. The classical prestige of the Book of Odes and the imperial status of the calligrapher have contributed to the great fame of these works, of which the Boston scroll is a splendid example.

Plate 98 illustrates *Heavy Dew*, an ode which was thought to refer to the ruler's entertaining of guests; plate 99 illustrates the ode, *On the Southern Hills Grow the T'ai Plants*.

Published: Kojiro Tomita and A. Kaiming Chiu, "Scroll of Six Odes from Mao Shih," *MFA Bulletin*, L, 281 (1952), 41–49.

100
Chu Ta (ca. 1625–after 1705)
Lotus in the manner of Hsü Wei
China, Ch'ing period, 17th century
Ink on paper. H. 185 cm., W. 89.8 cm.
Keith McLeod Fund. 56.495

In this work the artist Chu Ta, better known by his sobriquet Pa-ta-shan-jên, follows the style of Hsü Wei (1521–1593), one of the great eccentrics of the Ming period who specialized in monochrome paintings of plants and birds. A strange and tortured personality himself, Chu Ta must have felt a close affinity to Hsü Wei.

Continuing the tradition established by Hsü Wei the artist created his monochrome lotuses and birds in endless variations. To what extent these should be interpreted allegorically remains an open question. The poem inscribed on this painting, although difficult to understand, seems to contain an oblique reference to the fall of the Ming dynasty. Chu Ta was a distant relative of the Ming house and the fall of the dynasty constituted a tragic turning point in his life, to which he often refers in his work.

Published: Kojiro Tomita and Hsien-ch'i Tseng, *Portfolio of Chinese Paintings in the Museum (Yüan to Ch'ing Periods)*, Boston, 1961, Pl. 121.

101
Yakṣī
India, Sanchi, ca. 25 B.C.
Buff sandstone. H. 72 cm.
Denman Waldo Ross Collection. 29.999

This torso of a tree-dryad (*yakṣī*) originally served as a bracket figure on one of the gateways *(toraṇa)*, probably the south, of the great Buddhist stūpa at Sanchi. At this period the Buddhists enriched their artistic repertoire by incorporating into their work themes and motifs prevalent in secular as well as religious life. Technically, this torso exemplifies the artist's complete understanding of the structural elements of the female form and its sculptural possibilities. The peculiarly Indian artistic approach to the human form—to envision it as abstraction without, however, distilling its sensuous grace—is apparent in this elegant lady. Although the modeling is confined to the essential planes, the figure, which is carved fully in the round, conveys a feeling for naturalism and sensuousness seldom surpassed by later Indian sculptors. The ample breasts, the luxuriant hips, and the prominent pelvis symbolize the yakṣī's function as a fertility spirit. The treatment of the long tresses on the back, falling down to the hip, is as simple and effective as the girdle that accentuates her nudity.

Published: H. Zimmer, *The Art of Indian Asia*, New York, 1955, Vol. 2, Pl. 22; J. Rosenfield, "The Arts of Buddhist India," *MFA Bulletin*, LXIII, 333 (1965), 156–157, figs. 4 and 4a; B. Rowland, *The Art and Architecture of India*, 3rd ed., Harmondsworth, 1967, Pl. 23.

102
DancingRailing Pillar with Two Figures
India, Mathura, 2nd century A.D.
Mottled red sandstone. H. 56.4 cm.
Black Fund. 35.647

Railing pillar from a stairway showing two figures, a woman with a flaming torch, and a male peering over a draped hanging. Perhaps the subject represents a heroine setting forth to a rendezvous *(abhisārikā nāyikā)*, watched by a mischievous servant. Such "Peeping Tom" scenes were particularly popular with Mathura artists, who delighted in rendering amusing themes. The Mathura school inherited the Sanchi tradition of delineating the female form with abundance and grace, emphasizing the essential elements of the physical form. At this time Mathura was a prolific center of art, especially under the patronage of the imperial Kuṣāṇas, catering to the taste of a rich mercantile community and to diverse religious establishments. A motif such as this, however, was part of a universal vocabulary that the artist frequently employed, irrespective of the sectarian affiliation of the monument.

Published: J. Rosenfield, "The Arts of Buddhist India," *MFA Bulletin*, LXIII, 333 (1965), 150, fig. 14.

103
Avalokiteśvara
India, Sarnath, 6th century
Buff sandstone. H. 30 cm.
Helen and Alice Colburn Fund. 34.229

Although fragmentary, the effigy of the Thathāgata Amitābha on the crown establishes the identification of the figure with the Bodhisattva Avalokiteśvara. The concept of the Bodhisattva is perhaps the most significant contribution of the Mahāyāna school to Buddhist thought. A Bodhisattva is a being who postpones his own *nirvāṇa* in order to liberate other sentient beings. Avalokiteśvara is the Bodhisattva *par excellence* responsible for looking after the world until the arrival of Maitreya, the Buddha of the future. This work reveals the delicacy with which the Sarnath artists handled their material, particularly in rendering details. Compassion is the primary quality of Avalokiteśvara and it is well expressed in the benign and smiling countenance. The form is defined with sober elegance in the best Sarnath manner.

Published: J. Rosenfield, "The Arts of Buddhist India," *MFA Bulletin*, LXIII, 333 (1965), 156, fig. 21.

104
Dancing Apsaras
Cambodia, 11th century
Bronze. H. 39.3 cm.
Denman Waldo Ross Collection. 22.686

The elegant apsaras dances on a lotus springing from the stem of a flowering spray which terminates in a half-open bud, revealing a similar but hieratic female figure, holding a flower in each hand. The danseuse's hands touch a flame-fringed trifoliate arch which springs from dragon bases. She is elaborately ornamented and crowned, although the torso is bare. A remarkably alive and animated bronze, it expresses the sinuous and lyrical qualities of the Khmer style. The piece is conceived as an organic design of great charm and elegance, showing the rhythmic rapport between the human form and nature.

Published: A. Coomaraswamy, *Catalogue of the Indian Collections in the Museum of Fine Arts, Part II, Sculpture*, Boston, 1923, Pl. XXXII; A. Coomaraswamy, *History of Indian and Indonesian Art*, New York, 1927, Pl. CXIX, p. 365; B. Rowland, *The Art and Architecture of India*, 3rd ed., Harmondsworth, 1967, Pl. 162.

105
Amitābha with Acolytes
Nepal, 12th–13th century
Gouache on cloth. H. 41.3 cm., W. 33 cm.
Gift of John Goelet. 67.818

The crowned figure in the center is the Tathāgata Amitābha. He is flanked by the Bodhisattvas, Maitreya and Avalokiteśvara, while six others are seated on either side of his head. Other Tathāgatas and divinities of the Vajrayāna pantheon are represented along the top and the bottom. The painting seems to represent the mandala of the eight great Bodhisattvas, the earliest representation of which is to be found in Ellora. The concept of the eight Bodhisattvas evidently enjoyed special favor in Central Asia, Nepal, and Tibet at this period. This work is one of the earliest known Nepali paintings and is very closely related stylistically to illuminations in dated eleventh and twelfth century manuscripts. Although the composition is determined by the iconography, it remains a masterpiece of Nepali painting both in the refinement of the drawing and in the soft tonality of the colors.

106

DARBAR OF JAHANGIR
India, Mughal, ca. A.D. 1620
Gouache on paper. H. 34.5 cm., W. 19.5 cm.
Goloubew Collection. Francis Bartlett Donation of 1912 and Picture Fund. 14.654

The painting represents the Darbar of Jahangir in the Diwan-i-khas at Agra. The important courtiers present are all named in inscriptions, and the scene is, perhaps, a graphic record of the Emperor's audience to Prince Parviz in 1619. The signature declares it to be a "work of the humble house-born [artists]." It has been suggested that the artists involved were Abu'l Hasan and Manohar. The solemnity of the formal occasion is evident from the faces of the courtiers, and the entire composition, with the Emperor at the apex of the pyramid, evokes the majesty and grandeur of an imperial court. The drawing of the faces reveals the degree of perfection achieved by Mughal artists in profile portraiture. Due largely to Jahangir's passionate interest in painting, the Mughal style reached its apogee during his reign. This miniature is an outstanding example of the imperial Mughal tradition.

Published: A. Coomaraswamy, *Les Miniatures Orientales de la Collection Goloubew*, Paris and Brussels, 1929, Pl. LXXII, fig. 122; A. Coomaraswamy, *Catalogue of the Indian Collections in the Museum of Fine Arts, Part VI, Mughal Painting*, Boston, 1930, Pl. XXXIV, p. 44; S. C. Welch, *The Art of Mughal India*, New York, 1963, Pl. 30.

107

POET IN A GARDEN
India, Deccan, ca. A.D. 1610
Gouache on paper. H. 12.2 cm., W. 10.3 cm.
Goloubew Collection. Francis Bartlett Donation of 1912 and Picture Fund. 14.663

The poet is seated before a cherry tree in a garden with books, inkstand, and flask. The signature at the back is of Mir 'Imad Husaini, who was a famous calligrapher working under Shah Abbas and who died in A.D. 1615. A strong Persian influence is apparent in the landscaping, particularly in the rendering of the cherry tree and flowers and in the manner in which the figure is disposed. Although it is

generally considered to be a Mughal miniature, recently it has been attributed to Golconda in the Deccan, which is not unlikely. Whatever the provenance, it is a charming painting revealing exceptionally delicate drawing. The face of the poet is particularly expressive.

Published: A. Coomaraswamy, *Les Miniatures Orientales de la Collection Goloubew*, Paris and Brussels, 1929, Pl. LXX, p. 119; A. Coomaraswamy, *Catalogue of the Indian Collections in the Museum of Fine Arts, Part VI, Mughal Painting*, Pl. XXV, p. 35; D. Barrett and B. Gray, *Painting of India*, Skira, 1963, p. 125.

108

ŚAṬHA NĀYAKA OR THE FALSE GALLANT
India, Basohli, ca. A.D. 1690
Gouache on paper. H. 23.4 cm., W. 33.4 cm.
Ross-Coomaraswamy Collection. 17.2780

The gallant of blue complexion is attempting to loosen the knot of the heroine's skirt. Here the hero obviously represents Kṛṣṇa, and the heroine probably Rādhā. A quotation at the back describes the scene eloquently:
Showing her a beautiful girdle, drawing on a fair
    panel with red chalk, putting a bracelet
    on her wrists and laying a necklace on her breasts,
Wishing the confidence of the fawn-eyed lady of fair brows,
    he slyly loosens the knot of her skirt below the girdle-
    stead, with naughty hand. (A.K.C.)
The painting is from a series illustrating a treatise on *nāyakabheda*. The architectural setting is typical of the Basohli style of the period. The colors are vivid and warm, and the artist has used silver and beetle wings to enliven the visual effect.

Published: A Coomaraswamy, *Catalogue of the Indian Collections in the Museum of Fine Arts, Part V, Rājput Painting*, Boston, 1930, Pl. XCII, p. 171.

109

KṚṢṆA AND RĀDHĀ SHELTERING FROM THE RAIN
India, Garhwal or Kangra, late 18th century
Gouache on paper. H. 29.7 cm., W. 21.1 cm.
Ross-Coomaraswamy Collection. 17.2614

Kṛṣṇa and Rādhā, along with others, are taking shelter from the rain under a cloak in a grove. One of the cowherds is rather humorously portrayed within the crevice in a tree, while another holds a leaf over his head. The two lovers, however, seem oblivious of the rain as they gaze into each other's eyes. Despite its idyllic quality, the miniature records an incident that often occurs during the monsoons, when a sudden shower drives people to find improvised shelter. The soft tones of the colors, especially the muted greens, not only convey the freshness of the landscape after the early rains, but help to better express the tender mood of love.

Published: A. Coomaraswamy, *Catalogue of the Indian Collections in the Museum of Fine Arts, Part V, Rājput Painting*, Boston, 1930, Pl. LXXXI, p. 161; W. Lillys, R. Reiff, E. Esin, *Oriental Miniatures*, Rutland (Vermont) and Tokyo, 1965, pp. 60–61.

110

LEAF OF A SHĀHNĀMA, SHOWING THE BATTLE OF ALEXANDER WITH THE DRAGON
Persia, Mongol period, 14th century
Gouache on paper. H. 17.5 cm., W. 29.2 cm.
Denman Waldo Ross Collection. 30.105

This leaf with its miniature is from a manuscript of the Persian epic, the *Shāhnāma*, popularly known as the *Demotte Shāhnāma*. The legend above the miniature reads "Combat of Alexander and the Rhinoceros." The dragon, a composite of rhinoceros, wolf, lion, and eagle, is an inventive elaboration of the text's description of a fire-breathing creature. Alexander, followed by his army, is about to strike the dragon with his sword. A number of different stylistic influences are apparent in this painting. The landscape, derived from Sung sources in China, is nonetheless Iranian in feeling, while the figures and the color (including the gold sky) reflect more than an awareness of Mesopotamian and Byzantine models. All these influences, however, are assimilated here into an original and dramatic style worthy of the heroic theme. This and other illustrations of the *Demotte Shāhnāma* constitute by far the greatest works of Persian painting of the fourteenth century.

Published: A. Coomaraswamy, "Miniatures from an Early Persian Shāh Nāmah," *MFA Bulletin*, XXVIII, 166 (1930), 26 ff.; B. Gray, *Persian Painting*, Skira, 1961, p. 28.

111

Arraji Muhammad al Qawan
A TRIUMPHANT ENTRY, FROM A MANUSCRIPT OF THE SHĀHNĀMA
Turkey, A.D. 1552–1585
Full color and gold on paper. H. 33 cm., W. 47.5 cm. (each leaf)
Goloubew Collection. Francis Bartlett Donation of 1912 and Picture Fund. 14.691

This large double page composition vividly records a triumphal procession about to enter a city. The Persian text on the painting is in honor of the Sultan, who may have been either Murad III or Salim II, both contemporaries of Arraji Muhammad. It may be mentioned that these leaves

are from the same manuscript as the leaf with calligraphy (Pl. 112), and Arraji Muhammad was both the painter and the calligrapher. Although these are considered examples of miniature painting, the composition attains a monumentality and grandeur worthy of a mural. The artist has handled the groupings of the figures with great facility, and the drawing is especially articulate and refined. In the colophon Arraji Muhammad declares that "the aim of this painting is that something should remain of us"; he could hardly have left behind a more eloquent memorial.

Published: A. Coomaraswamy, *Les Miniatures Orientales de la Collection Goloubew*, Paris and Brussels, 1929, pp. 60–62, Pls. LIV–LVII.

112

Arraji Muhammad al Qawan
LEAF OF A SHĀHNĀMA
Turkey, A.D. 1552–1585
Ink and color on paper. H. 33 cm., W. 47.5 cm.
Goloubew Collection. Francis Bartlett Donation of 1912 and Picture Fund. 14.692

Islam has always held the art of writing in high esteem, which resulted in a richly developed tradition of calligraphy in all Islamic countries. This particular page, containing the last part of the text and colophons of a *Shāhnāma* manuscript, was written by Arraji Muhammad al Qawan between A.D. 1552–1585. That Arraji Muhammad was an accomplished master is evident from the fluent and refined quality of his style. The writing, either in black or white along the margin, is set off against bands of gold, blues, pink, or orange, and ornamented with delicate floral designs, evidently to match the brightness of the miniature on contiguous folios.

113

BULL'S HEAD
Persia, 12th century
Gold. H. 4.6 cm., W. 4.1 cm.
Annie Louise Richards Fund. 25.584

This gold ornament comes from a grave in Tehran. It is made in a granular technique which was used as early as the Sumerian era; the bull itself is an ancient motif. Despite its diminutive size, there is great character in the face of the bull; the artist, perhaps in whimsy, gave it drooping ears and soulful eyes.

114

STATUETTE OF A MAN
Persia, 12th century

Gold. H. 6.6 cm., W. 3.6 cm.
Annie Louise Richards Fund. 25.583

This statuette is of a bearded man with drooping moustache; he is wearing a regal cloak. Like the Bull's Head (Pl. 113), this too comes from a grave in Tehran and was made in the granular technique. It probably represents a king and may even be the effigy of the person to whose grave it belonged.

115
VASE
Persia, Gurgan (?), 10th–12th century
Glass. H. 9 cm., D. 7 cm.
Gift of the John Goelet Foundation. 65.241

The vase is of thick, honey-colored glass showing heavy iridescence, perhaps owing to burial in the earth. The principal element of design is the use of a facet pattern in three stages: eight facets above, fifteen below, and nine on the solid foot. This facet pattern was probably achieved by molding as was usually the case with Islamic glass before the thirteenth century. Its strong but simple shape imparts to it an elegance that makes it especially attractive.

116
BOWL
Persia, Nishapur, 10th century
Pottery. H. 8.3 cm., D. 21.7 cm.
Keith McLeod Fund. 65.1278

The principle decorative theme is a horse and a rider, a theme more familiar in the wares of Rayy than Nishapur. Both the rider and the horse are highly stylized, although the cavalier with his arms outstretched has a heraldic presence. His right hand holds the reins of the horse and the left a flowering stem. The remaining part of the interior of the bowl is filled with birds and floral motifs. On the outside, the upper part of the bowl is decorated with vertical lozenge-shaped motifs. The principle colors are yellow, green, and dark brown on buff.

117
BOWL
Persia, Kashan, early 13th century
Pottery. H. 7.9 cm., D. 18.6 cm.
Mary S. and Edward J. Holmes Fund. 65.1668

This deep bowl is ornamented with a vine and leaf arabesque design, which is painted in black under brilliant torquoise glaze. The rim and the exterior are somewhat iridescent. The delicate and attractive design makes this one of the finest examples of Kashan ware. Kashan was particularly active in the manufacture of this sort of ware in the early thirteenth century, and the potters created a decorative style of simple elegance.

118
CANDELABRUM
Egypt, mid 14th century
Brass, inlaid with silver and gold. H. 35.6 cm.
Ellen Frances Mason Fund. 34.168

The large Nashki script between two medallions with radiating script is set off by a background of rich floral arabesque. The perimeter of the medallions is filled in with stylized birds intricately intertwined with tendrils. In narrower bands along the top and the bottom are shown a great variety of prancing animals, foliage, and rosettes. The refined and exquisite workmanship of the candelabrum probably indicates that it was commissioned for a palace or an important mosque. Although the Islamic artists, especially in their metalwork, reveal a penchant for austere and geometrical forms combined with sinuous floral designs, the animals and birds in this example are rendered with remarkable naturalism.

119
THE BODHISATTVA'S BATH IN THE NAIRAÑJANA RIVER
India, Amaravati, 1st century. A.D.
Greenish limestone. H. 1.6 m., W. 1 m., DEPTH 14.5 cm.
Denman Waldo Ross Collection. 29.151

This fragment was used originally as part of an enclosing wall. The scene shows the bath of the Bodhisattva, Siddhārtha—who is represented symbolically by footprints—in the Nairañjana river. Indra is seen bowing before the footprints and on the other side are the Nāga king Kālika and his two wives. This was the occasion when Kālika had predicted the Bodhisattva's future enlightenment. Above are the four river goddesses, each bearing a vase of plenty. The schematic arrangement of the figures in tiers, the synoptic method of narration, and the emphasis on direct visual communcation are all typical features of early Buddhist bas-reliefs. However, by emphasizing the diagonal in the disposition of the arms and legs of the females in the upper register, the artist has made his composition more animated than most early Buddhist narrative art. As is characteristic of the Amaravati school, the slender and sumptuous figures seem to belong to a world that believes not in the austere metaphysics of renunciation but in the spontaneous joys of living.

Published: A. Coomaraswamy, "Andhra Sculptures," *MFA Bulletin*, XXVII, 160 (1929), 20 ff.; J. Rosenfield, "The Arts of Buddhist India," *MFA Bulletin*, LXIII, 333 (1965), 142.

120

THE RIVER GODDESS GAṄGĀ
India, Besnagar, ca. A.D. 500
Buff sandstone. H. 73.5 cm., W. 39.3 cm., DEPTH 15.4 cm.
Charles Amos Cummings Bequest Fund. 26.26

An architectural section showing the river goddess Gaṅgā, standing gracefully on her vehicle, the makara. A dwarf in heroic posture is busy extracting gems from the makara's mouth, while another stands reverently on its tail. Above is a mango tree, perhaps symbolizing abundance. This is an elegant example of Gupta sculpture, vividly displaying the characteristics of the style: clarity and balance in the composition, abstract but sensuous modeling of the figures, the articulate definition of the form by fluid outline, and the ideal proportions that remains the "classical" standard for later Indian art.

Published: A. Coomaraswamy, *History of Indian and Indonesian Art*, New York, 1927, Pl. XLVII, fig. 177; H. Zimmer, *The Art of Indian Asia*, New York, 1955, Vol. 2, fig. 105c; J. Rosenfield, "The Arts of Buddhist India," *MFA Bulletin*, LXIII, 333 (1965), 159, fig. 23.

121

GAUTAMA BUDDHA
India, Bezwada (?), 6th century
Bronze. H. 50.3 cm.
Gift of the Government Museum, Madras. 21.1504

The figure is a classic example in metal of the Buddha image in the mature Gupta style. With assured elegance the left hand gathers the end of the robes, which leaves the right shoulder and arm bare and free. All the auspicious signs of greatness *(mahāpuruṣa-lakṣaṇa)* such as the curly hair, the cranial bump, the extended earlobes, etc. are fully developed. The bronze is probably from Buddhapad near Bezwada, an area that was still very active in Buddhism in the sixth century. The modeling and proportions of the figure, the graceful *déhanchement*, the shape of the face, the half-shut eyes symbolizing introspection, and the full lips clearly reflect the pervading influence of the Sarnath school. Such images were responsible for transporting the Indian styles to other South Asian countries.

Published: A. Coomaraswamy, *Catalogue of the Indian Collections in the Museum of Fine Arts, Part II, Sculpture*, Boston, 1923, Pl. XXI; A. Coomaraswamy, *History of Indian and Indonesian Art*, New York, 1927, Pl. XL, fig. 159; J. Rosenfield, "The Arts of Buddhist India," *MFA Bulletin*, LXIII, 333 (1965), 153, fig. 17.

122

BUDDHA WITH TWO ATTENDANT BODHISATTVAS
India, Kashmir, 8th century
Ivory. H. 12.2 cm.
Charles B. Hoyt, Marshall H. Gould, and John Ware Willard Funds. 63.1495

The Buddha is seated in the yogic posture *(paryaṅkāsana)* between two attendant Bodhisattvas. As is typical of Kashmiri Buddhist art of the post-Gupta period, the sculpture shows iconographic influences of both the Mathura and the Gandhāra schools. However, the Gupta ideal of a smooth, leonine torso with a concise and sober definition of the form has been retained. The physiognomy is characteristically Kashmiri. The folds of the garments are extremely stylized, and together with the lively delineation of the attendant figures, they imbue the ivory with considerable verve and animation.

Published: M. C. Beach, "Two Indian Ivories Newly Acquired," *MFA Bulletin*, LXII, 329 (1964), 95 ff.

123

DURGĀ AS THE SLAYER OF THE BUFFALO DEMON
India, Pallava, 8th century
Dark granulite. H. 1.5 cm.
Denman Waldo Ross Collection. 27.171

The goddess with eight arms stands triumphant in graceful *déhanchement (tribhaṅga)* on the head of the buffalo demon whom she has destroyed. Among the recognizable attributes are the trident, the sword, the discus, and the arrow in the right hands; and the shield, the conch, and the bow in the left. In her emanation as Mahiṣāsuramarddinī, Durgā is worshipped in India as the symbol of Primordial Energy, triumphing over evil personified by the demon. The sculpture is a superb example of the Pallava style that had matured by the late seventh century as is apparent from the Mamallapuram monuments. The Pallava artists developed a sophisticated artistic idiom of their own which combined the earlier Andhra tradition of slim and elegantly proportioned figures with a dynamic vitality that was probably inspired by the Hindu themes.

Published: A. Coomaraswamy, "A Pallava Relief, Durgā," *MFA Bulletin*, XXV, 148 (1927), 22 ff., fig. 27; B. Rowland, *The Art and Architecture of India*, 3rd ed., Harmondsworth, 1967, fig. 116.

124

VIŚVARŪPA VIṢṆU
Nepal, 9th century
Gilt copper. H. 30.8 cm.

Keith McLeod Fund from the Nasli and Alice Heeramaneck Collection. 67.5

The ten-armed god stands firm like a column on a plain pedestal. He wears a *dhoti* of printed design, held with a girdle, a necklace, earrings, an elaborate crown with the face of glory *(kīrttimukha)*, a sacred thread, and bracelets designed as serpents. His attributes are the lotus seed, battle-axe, sword, discus, elephant goad, bow, shield, mace, and conch. The back of the figure is as richly finished as the front, the ten arms emerging coherently from the shoulders, and the hair falling over the neck in stylized but well-groomed curls. With his ten arms, the god here reveals his universal form *(viśvarūpa)*, described so eloquently in the *Bhagavad-Gītā*. Bronze casting was already a developed art in Nepal by the seventh century as attested by visiting Chinese dignitaries, and this superb bronze shows the technical dexterity of the Newari artist in this field.

Published: P. Pal, ''Vaisṇava Sculpture From Nepal,'' *MFA Bulletin*, LXV, 340 (1967), 46–47.

125

ŚĀNTINĀTHA
India, Akota, 10th century
Bronze. H. 24.3 cm.
Marshall H. Gould Fund. 62.928

The seated figure with his hands in the gesture of meditation *(samādhimudrā)* represents the Jaina Tīrthaṅkara, Śāntinātha. His distinctive emblems are two deer confronting the wheel. He is flanked by his exclusive yakṣa and yakṣī attendants, Kimpuruṣa and Mahāmānasī. As is usual in bronzes portraying Jaina themes, the abstract and concise modeling—almost geometric in its precision—of the main figures well expresses the austere metaphysics of the Jaina philosophy. Despite its modest size, the bronze is endowed with heroic quality and inherent majesty.

126

MAHĀVĪRA
Central India, 10th-11th century
Buff sandstone. H. 77 cm.
Denman Waldo Ross Collection. 29.1001

Mahāvīra is seated in the yogic posture *(paryaṅkāsana)*, his hands displaying the gesture of meditation *(samādhimudrā)*. To his right is his attendant yakṣa, Mātaṅga, and a female devotee. On either side of his head are celestial figures engaged in adoration, while the umbrella of majesty is upheld by two elephants. Mahāvīra is the last of the twenty-four Jaina Tīrthankaras but undoubtedly the greatest. The hieratic frontality and the symmetrical

composition are determined by the function of the sculpture, which served as a cult icon to be viewed only from the front. Isolated as such sculptures are from their original habitat, it is difficult to suggest an exact school. In general, this work displays the characteristics of the sculpture of Central India of about the tenth to eleventh century.

127

LOKANĀTHA
India, Bihar, 11th century
Gray schist. H. 88.9 cm.
Marshall H. Gould and Frederick L. Jacks Fund. 63.418

Seated in princely posture the Bodhisattva holds a lotus stem with his left hand; the right hand, now broken, probably displayed the gesture of exposition *(vyākhyānamudrā)*. The Tathāgata on the matted crown is Amitābha, his spiritual father, as Lokanātha is another manifestation of Avalokiteś-vara (see Pl. 103). A work of the mature Pāla style, the sculpture is probably from the Bishenpur-Tandawa region of Bihar (see R. D. Banerji, *Eastern Indian School of Medieval Sculpture*, Delhi, 1933, Pl. XXXLL). The extreme sway and rhythmic motion of the body are here arrested by the articulate and mellifluent outline. Stylistically, the sculpture represents the transition between the soft but crisp and taut modeling of the mature Pāla style and the langorous but effete grace of later works of the Sena period.

128

MODEL CART WITH TWO BULLOCKS
India, Chanhu-daro (Sind), Harappa Culture,
2nd millenium B.C.
Reddish-buff clay with red slip. L. 8.4 cm.
Joint Expedition of the American School of Indic and Iranian Studies and the Museum of Fine Arts, 1935–1936 Season. 36.2231–35

Such model bullock-carts were probably used as toys for children. The bulls display acute observation and sympathetic rendering of the natural form of the animal, a typical characteristic of animal sculpture of Harappan culture. The cart represents a type that may still be seen on Indian roads today, exemplifying another facet of the remarkable continuity of Indian culture through five millennia.

129

HAWK ATTACKING A DUCK
Persia, Rayy, 10th–11th century
Stucco. H. 31.2 cm.
University Museum—Museum of Fine Arts Persian Expedition. 35.915

This stucco, presumably used as a wall decoration, was found during the Persian expedition at Rayy (six miles southeast of Tehran) in the Buwaihid-Seljuq layer. It represents a hawk pouncing upon the neck of an unfortunate duck. Although the birds are rendered conceptually, it is obvious that the artist has observed the situation in nature. The entire composition reflects a strong sense of design in the way the outlines of the two birds flow into each other. The symbolism of such motifs in an Islamic context is still undetermined, but they seem to have been popular in the Mediterranean world for they frequently occur in Byzantine art as far west as Greece.

130

ELEPHANT
Persia, Gurgan (?), 12th century
Pottery. H. 33.9 cm., W. 23 cm.
Keith McLeod Fund. 65.1271

This elephant with howdah, rider, and driver was painted with black under turquoise glaze and engraved. Such elephants are rather rare in Persian ceramics and this is an outstanding example of a ceramic object whose function was purely decorative. The animal is modeled almost in abstract volumes. Although the legs are straight and pillar-like, and the head and trunk rather disproportionate, the artist has well expressed the sense of volume and elemental power of the animal. The summary modeling is also apparent in the two seated figures which seem to reflect a primitive or folk tradition.

131

BOWL
Persia, late 12th–early 13th century
Pottery, Minai ware. H. 8.5 cm., D. 20.5 cm.
Gift of Miss Helen Norton in memory of Harry A. Norton. 63.1391

The main part of the bowl is occupied by a king seated on a throne and accompanied by four attendants. Other decorative motifs include floriate arches, two birds, and along the inner rim edge an abstract design of blue-gray, white, and brown, derived probably from script. There is an inscription on the outside of the bowl. The bowl is painted in polychrome enamel with gilding on white ground, but, typical of the early Minai ware, the colors—purple, green, blue, and gray—are soft and muted. The piece does not have a glazed sheen, but the surface shows a smooth and fine texture.

132

EWER
Persia, early 13th century
Brass, inlaid with silver. H. 41.8 cm.
The Holmes Collection. 49.1901

The body of this noble ewer is fluted in ten vertical lobes and richly inlaid with silver. The high curving lip-spout has a hinged cover; the sides of the neck show crouching lions with fully rounded heads. Below, the raised ring of silver is decorated with lions chasing hares. Harpies back-to-back ornament the rim, and musicians the shoulder. Around the body is a frieze of arch-shaped medallions with festival scenes; there is a benedictory Nashki inscription on the neck and the base. The delicacy of the design and the refinement of the inlay work make this one of the finest examples of Islamic inlaid metalwork.

133

'Abdullah ibn al-Fadl
LEAF OF ARABIC TRANSLATION OF THE MATERIA MEDICA OF DIOSCORIDES
Iraq, Baghdad, A.D. 1224 (A.H. 621)
Gouache on paper. H. 25 cm., W. 33 cm.
Goloubew Collection, Francis Bartlett Donation of 1912 and Picture Fund. 14.536

Two physicians (apothecaries) stand on either side of a large jar and discuss the preparation of medicine. Both are provided with halos, one wears blue robes and the other red. To judge from the large number of illustrated copies in existence, the *Materia Medica* seems to have been a popular treatise with the Arabs at the time. The illustrations were added as graphic explanations of the texts; their strongly figurative style goes back to Hellenistic and Byzantine models, but the delineation is more free and lively. The function of these miniatures is purely explanatory: the composition is simple and the bold colors against the neutral background make a direct visual appeal.
  Published: MFA Bulletin, XIII, 74 (1915), 2.

134

VIBHĀSA RĀGIṆĪ
India, Malwa, ca. A.D. 1640
Gouache on paper. H. 19.2 cm., W. 14.2 cm.
Ross-Coomaraswamy Collection. 17.2382

This painting is from a Rāgāmālā set and portrays the musical mode (*rāgiṇī*), Vibhāsa, which is personified as a lady seated on a bed with her lover. The lover shoots a flower arrow at a crowing cock perched on the leaves of a plantain tree. The cock is obviously the harbinger of dawn, and the lover, wishing not to be disturbed, is chasing it away. The painting belongs to a set of several others, portraying musical modes. The miniatures of this set are characterized by few figures, usually placed within an architectural context, a deep blue-black background, and simplicity and economy in the composition.

 Published: A. Coomaraswamy, *Catalogue of the Indian Collections in the Museum of Fine Arts, Part V, Rājput Painting*, Boston, 1930, p. 77, Pl. VIII.

A Selected Bibliography

BELL, HAMILTON. "Early Chinese Paintings in the Museum of Fine Arts, Boston," *Art in America*, V (1917), 117–130, 168–180, 221–231.

BROOKS, VAN WYCK. *Fenollosa and His Circle*. New York, 1962.

(The) Charles B. Hoyt Collection, Memorial Exhibition, Feb. 13–Mar. 30, 1952. Boston, 1952.

CHISOLM, LAWRENCE W. *Fenollosa: The Far East and American Culture*. New Haven, 1963.

COBURN, FREDERICK W. "Chinese Stone Sculpture at Boston," *Burlington Magazine*, XX (1911) 12 ff.

COOMARASWAMY, ANANDA K. *Portfolio of Indian Art*. New York, 1923.
—. *Catalogue of the Indian Collections in the Museum of Fine Arts, Boston, Part I, General Introduction. Part II, Sculpture*. Boston, 1923; *Part IV, Jaina Paintings and Manuscripts*. Boston, 1924; *Part V, Rājput Painting*. Boston, 1926; *Part VI, Mughal Painting*. Boston, 1930
—. *The Treatise of Al-Jazarī on Automata*. Boston, 1924.
—. *Les Miniatures Orientales de la Collection Goloubew au Museum of Fine Arts de Boston*. (*Ars Asiatica*, XIII) Paris and Brussels, 1929.

EASTMAN, ALVIN CLARK. *The Nala-Damayantī Drawings*. Boston, 1959.

FENOLLOSA, ERNEST F. *Epochs of Chinese and Japanese Art*. I and II, New York and London, 1912; new edition 1913.

KISHIDA TSUTOMU, "Bosuton Bijutsukan shūshū no Nihon Kaiga chōsa hōkoku ("A Survey of the Collection of Japanese Painting in the Boston Museum," text in Japanese), *Saga Daigaku Kyōikubu Kenkyūrombunshū*, Part I (Ashikaga Idealistic School), 15 (1965), 85–117; Part II (Post Ashikaga Idealistic School), 14 (1966), 77–96; Part III (Kano School), 15 (1967), 105–135; [to be continued].

KÜMMEL, OTTO. "Ostasiatische Malerei im Museum of Fine Arts in Boston," *Zeitschift für Bildende Kunst*, Band XXI, Heft 2, Nov. 1910.

MACKAY, ERNEST J. H. *Chanhu-Daro Excavations, 1935–36*. New Haven, 1943.

MORSE, EDWARD SYLVESTER. *Catalogue of the Morse Collection of Japanese Pottery*. Cambridge, 1901.

Museum of Fine Arts Bulletin, 1903– .

OKABE KAKUYA. *Japanese Sword Guards*. Boston, 1908.
—. *Special Exhibition of Sword Guards*. Boston, 1907.

PAINE, ROBERT TREAT, JR. *Catalogue of a Special Exhibition of Japanese Screen Paintings: Birds, Flowers and Animals; From the Collection in the Museum of Fine Arts, Boston*. Boston, 1935.
—. *Catalogue of a Special Exhibition of Japanese Screen Paintings: Landscapes and Figures; From the Collection in the Museum of Fine Arts, Boston*. Boston, 1938.
—. *Ten Japanese Paintings*. Privately printed for The Japan Society of New York, 1939.
—. *Figure Compositions of China and Japan, From the Collection of the Museum of Fine Arts, Boston*. Boston, 1964.

PAL, PRATAPADITYA. *Rāgamālā Paintings in the Museum of Fine Arts, Boston*. Boston, 1967.

TOMITA, KOJIRO. *Portfolio of Chinese Paintings in the Museum (Han to Sung Periods)*. Cambridge, 1933; 2nd ed. 1938.
—. *Day and Night in the Four Seasons: Sketches by Hokusai, 1760–1849*. Boston, 1957.
—. "Bosuton Bijutsukan Gojūnen" ("Fifty years in the Boston Museum," text in Japanese), *Geijutsu Shinchō*, IX, 8 (1958), 278 ff.
— and HSIEN-CH'I TSENG. *Portfolio of Chinese Paintings in the Museum (Yüan to Ch'ing Periods)*. Boston, 1961.

TSENG, HSIEN-CH'I. *Chinese Art Treasures*. Boston, 1961.
— and ROBERT PAUL DART. *The Charles B. Hoyt Collection in the Museum of Fine Arts, Boston, I*. Boston, 1964.

WAYMAN, DOROTHY GODFREY. *Edward Sylvester Morse; A Biography*. Cambridge, 1942.

WETZEL, HERVEY, E. "Persian and Indian Paintings in the Museum of Fine Arts," *Art In America*, III (1915), 199–211, 284–299.